T0304090

Geology of Connemara in Western Ireland

The Connemara region in Western Ireland is world-renowned for its outstanding geology that is blended with spectacular landscapes. This book and its many colourful illustrations, maps, diagrams, field and landscape images detail the origin and formation of Connemara's metamorphic and igneous rocks in deep time from 700 to 380 million years ago. It combines many field geology observations and current research results, and describes the many geological processes involved in the formation of the bedrock foundations of Connemara: plate tectonics, granite magmatism, deformation, metamorphism and mineral deposits. An amazing book for students and geological societies that visit the region annually.

Features

- The only book available on the formation of the igneous and metamorphic rock complexes in Connemara
- Explores the regional geological context of Connemara from ~700 Ma to 385 Ma
- Incorporates the most up-to-date research results and many useful field images, maps and schematic diagrams for teachers and students alike
- Describes the deformation, metamorphic and magmatic histories in Pressure-Temperature-time (PTt) space
- Includes a chapter dedicated to the application of fluid inclusion studies to magmatic and hydrothermal mineralisation in the Galway Granite Complex and its environs

This book serves as a resource for professionals, academics and senior undergraduate and graduate students working and studying in the fields of geology, earth sciences and environmental sciences.

Geology of Connemara in Western Ireland

Unravelling the Region's Tectonic, Metamorphic and Magmatic Histories

Martin Feely

With the collaboration of
Alessandra Costanzo
Editing and Digital Artwork

CRC Press
Taylor & Francis Group
Boca Raton London New York

CRC Press is an imprint of the
Taylor & Francis Group, an **informa** business

Designed cover image: Looking NW from the granite lowlands towards the metamorphic highlands of Connemara. The granite ridge (~300m) on the left marks the northern boundary of the Galway Granite Batholith. The mountains beyond this ridge and those ranging across to the right edge of the image comprise The Twelve Bens(~580-700m), Lissoughter (~400m) and the Maumturk Mountains all representing the rocks of the Connemara Metamorphic Complex. The water body in the foreground is an inlet from Camus Bay located along Connemara's Atlantic Coastline.

Photograph taken on the western side of the Furnace Road (R336) approximately 1.75km to the N of Costelloe village. (GR: 53.313222,-9.552787)

First edition published 2025
by CRC Press
2385 NW Executive Center Drive, Suite 320, Boca Raton FL 33431

and by CRC Press
4 Park Square, Milton Park, Abingdon, Oxon, OX14 4RN

CRC Press is an imprint of Taylor & Francis Group, LLC

© 2025 Martin Feely

Library of Congress Cataloging-in-Publication Data
Names: Feely, Martin, author.
Title: A geology of Connemara in western Ireland : unravelling the region's tectonic, metamorphic, and magmatic histories / Martin Feely.
Description: First edition. | Boca Raton, FL : CRC Press, 2025. | Includes bibliographical references and index.
Identifiers: LCCN 2024007231 | ISBN 9781032698403 (hardback) | ISBN 9781032698427 (paperback) | ISBN 9781032698410 (ebook)
Subjects: LCSH: Geology--Ireland--Connemara.
Classification: LCC QE265 .F445 2025 | DDC 554.17/4--dc23/eng/20240509
LC record available at https://lccn.loc.gov/2024007231

ISBN: 978-1-032-69840-3 (hbk)
ISBN: 978-1-032-69842-7 (pbk)
ISBN: 978-1-032-69841-0 (ebk)

DOI: 10.1201/9781032698410

Typeset in Palatino
by SPi Technologies India Pvt Ltd (Straive)

To my wife, Kate

Contents

Foreword xi

Preface.. xii

Acknowledgements xiv

About the Author xv

1 **Introduction to the Geology of Connemara** 1
   Connemara: A Summary of Its Geographical Setting and Geology......... 1
   The Spatial Distribution of Connemara's Metamorphic and
   Igneous Rocks.. 4
   The Connemara Metamorphic Complex....................................... 4
      The Dalradian Metamorphosed Sedimentary and
      Igneous Rocks.. 4
      The Metagabbro Gneiss Suite (MGGS) 6
   The Galway Granite Complex 8
   Glacial Landscapes of Connemara 8
   References 12

2 **The Connemara Metamorphic Complex: Dalradian**
   Lithostratigraphy and the Metagabbro Gneiss Suite 14
   Introduction 15
   The Dalradian Rocks of the Northern Belt: Plate Tectonic
   Perspectives 15
   The Dalradian Lithostratigraphy... 18
      Clifden Schist Formation 19
      Connemara Marble Formation.. 20
      Barnanoraun Schist Formation 23
      The Cleggan Boulder Bed Formation.................................... 25
      Bennabeola Quartzite Formation... 26
      Streamstown Schist Formation 27
      The Lakes Marble Formation 28
      The Ballynakill Schist, Kylemore Schist and Cashel Schist
      Formations 29
      The Cornamona Marble Formation....................................... 31
      The Ben Levy Grit Formation... 32
      The Lough Kilbride Schist Formation................................... 32
      Geology and Topography Correlations 33
   The Southern Belt: The Metagabbro Gneiss Suite (MMGS) 33
      The Metagabbros... 35
      The Ortho- and Paragneisses.. 36
   References 38

3 **Deformation History of the Connemara Metamorphic Complex**...41
Introduction...41
The Northern Belt..43
The Southern Belt..47
The Delaney Dome and the Mannin Thrust.............................53
References...56

4 **Metamorphism of the Connemara Dalradian and the Metagabbro Gneiss Suite**.....................................59
Introduction...60
Metamorphism of the Connemara Dalradian Pelites...............60
The Migmatites and Granulites of the MGGS.........................66
The Connemara Marble Formation....................................68
Metabasites..71
Retrograde Metamorphism..71
References...73

5 **Deformation, Magmatism and Metamorphism in the CMC: Pressure-Temperature-time (P-T-t) Perspectives**.....................75
Introduction...75
The Relative Timing of Deformation, Magmatism and Metamorphism in the CMC.....................................78
Recent Recalculations of Previously Published Ages from the CMC.....................................78
A Series of Time-Related NW-SE Cross-Sections Tracking the Evolution of the CMC from ~472 to 462 Ma.....................78
The CMC and its Structural Setting in the Grampian Terrane of NW Ireland and Scotland.....................83
Pressure-Temperature-time (P-T-t) Paths.............................85
The Friedrich and Hodges (2016) P-T-t Path.........................85
The Yardley and Cliff (2022) Cur Hill-Maumeen P-T-t Path.....87
The Yardley and Cliff (2022) Lough Nahasleam Migmatites P-T-t Path.....................89
References...89

6 **The Galway Granite Complex (GGC): Geological Setting, Geochronology, Petrology, Geochemistry and Thermal Metamorphism**.....................92
The Geological Setting of the GGC.....................................92
The Geochronology of the GGC: Spatial and Temporal Relationships.....................................94

Introduction to the Petrology and Mineralogy of the GGC.....................95
Granite Classification: A Mineralogical Perspective...........................95
Geochemical Characteristics of the GGC 96
Thermal Metamorphism: Aureole Rocks of the GGC 98
References 99

7 **Structural Controls on the Assembly of the Galway Granite
   Complex**...103
   Iapetus Ocean Closure and Granite Magma Generation......................103
   Generation of the GGC's Magmas...104
   Structural Controls on the Ascent of the GGC's Magmas 106
   Ballooning and Block Stoping in the GGC................................ 110
   References 112

8 **The Plutons of the GGC: Emplacement, Field Relationships,
   Mineralogy and Petrology**... 115
   The Earlier Plutons 115
      The Omey Pluton 116
      The Inish Pluton 119
      The Roundstone Pluton...120
      The Letterfrack Pluton..122
   The Galway Batholith..123
   The Carna Pluton 123
   Feldspar Compositions in the Carna Pluton.............................129
   The Galway-Kilkieran Pluton 130
   The Granites of the Western and Eastern Blocks........................133
      The Western Block...133
      The Eastern Block...133
   The Granites of the Central Block.....................................135
   The Marginal Porphyritic Granodiorite (MPGr).........................136
   The Mafic Megacrystic Granodiorite (MMGr) 136
   The Mingling Mixing Zone Granodiorite (MMZGr).........................136
   The Lough Lurgan Granite (LLGr).......................................140
   The Knock Granite (KGr)...140
   The Shannapheasteen Granodiorite (ShGr) 140
   The Costelloe Murvey Granite (CMGr)...................................140
   Geochronometry of the Galway-Kilkieran Pluton.........................143
   Emplacement of the Galway-Kilkieran Pluton............................143
   Diking in the Galway Granite Complex..................................145
   References 145

9 **Magmatic and Hydrothermal Mineral Deposits in the
    Galway Granite Complex**..149
    Introduction 149
    The Molybdenite-Chalcopyrite (Mo-Cu) Mineralisation.......................150
    The Mo-Cu Mineralising Fluids: Insights from Fluid Inclusion
    Studies 153
    The Late Fluorite Polymineralic Veins in the GGC...............................154
    Late Fluorite Polymineralic Veins in the Connemara
    Metamorphic Complex 159
    References 160

Index...164

Foreword

By Professor John Parnell
School of Geosciences, Aberdeen, Scotland

You don't need to be a geologist to appreciate Connemara. The natural beauty and culture bring us to visit again and again. But the more that you understand the geology that creates the distinctive landscape, the visit can be elevated to a new level. And there's nobody better placed to guide you than Martin Feely.

Connemara is one of those special places on the edge of Europe where the complex history of the continental margin has thrown together rocks of many different ages. The result is perfect for teaching, and full of potential for research on geological phenomena. The example of Connemara takes us on a tour through time that includes a snowball Earth when the planet was frozen, a deep ocean with a stagnant seafloor, to a tropical shallow sea full of life. This journey of over 300 million years is only 30 km in modern Connemara. But it is the metamorphic rocks and granites that dominate the landscape, and which are the focus of this book. Martin describes their context, and then interrogates the rocks to tell us much about the processes involved in their formation and subsequent deformation. The wisdom gained from these rocks has proved key to understanding similar but less accessible rocks in many other parts of the world. This is why so many parties of geologists have come to see the rocks of Connemara and hear Martin tell their story.

Martin's knowledge of the region has been honed by a lifetime of teaching university students from Galway and taking visiting parties from elsewhere. The thousands who have passed through his hands and asked searching questions have helped to distil the knowledge in this book. It will, therefore, be an invaluable guide to geological visitors for many years to come. The decades of experience mean that he knows his patch intimately. If a key piece of evidence is a rock in a bog somewhere, Martin will be able to guide you to it. I know from experience that he can take you to the bit of featureless ground which hides the goods.

I've known Martin for over 30 years. It's always a pleasure to come to Galway and see the man and the mountains beyond. You can tell when a natural scientist enjoys his work, and Martin's love of this corner of Ireland shines through the pages. The book will go a long way to help you enjoy it also.

Preface

By Martin Feely

Emeritus Professor, School of Natural Sciences, University of Galway, Ireland.

The author has spent many decades teaching and researching the geological history of Connemara's landscapes. The results of his field and laboratory-based studies of the metamorphic and igneous rocks of Connemara have been published widely and have also been presented at numerous national and international geology conferences. His Connemara-based academic activities include lectures, summer schools and fieldtrips tailored for the national and international (the UK, Europe, Canada and the US) third-level education sectors, amateur groups and learned societies. The absence of a text that focuses specifically on the geology of the metamorphic and igneous complexes of Connemara suitable for these disparate groups inspired the author to produce this book. There are ten chapters; each chapter is illustrated using numerous images of Connemara's landscapes draped in their geological structures, its bedrock exposures, metamorphic and igneous rocks and minerals, and geology maps together with schematic models that focus on field relationships, deformation, metamorphism and granite magma generation, ascent and emplacement.

Chapter 1 describes the regional geology of the Connemara region. Chapters 2–4 describe the geological setting and petrology of the metamorphic rocks that comprise the Connemara Metamorphic Complex (CMC). Chapter 5 presents a detailed Pressure-Temperature-time (PTt) perspective for the plate tectonic assembly, deformation, magmatism and metamorphism of the Connemara Metamorphic Complex.

Chapters 6–9 detail the geology of the Galway Granite Complex (GGC) and describe the mineralogy and petrology of its individual plutons. The structures that controlled the construction of the complex are introduced in Chapter 7, with emphasis on the generation and ascent of the plutons that comprise the GGC. Chapter 8 details the field relationships, mineralogy, petrology, and the emplacement of each pluton. Finally, Chapter 9 describes the long-lived granite related molybdenite-chalcopyrite (Mo-Cu) mineralisation encountered throughout the GGC, and the later hydrothermal (Triassic?) vein deposits of fluorite (± chalcopyrite, galena, sphalerite, pyrite, calcite, quartz, and barite) that transect the metamorphic and igneous rocks of Connemara.

The book makes full use of maps, images and diagrams that illustrate the geological processes that have shaped Connemara's geology. Images of field localities used by the author, over the decades, to teach the mineralogy and petrology of Connemara's metamorphic and igneous bedrocks are featured throughout. The publication is designed to serve both as an introduction to the geology of Connemara and as a companion book that can be brought into Connemara and used as a field guide.

Acknowledgements

I wish to acknowledge the many mentors and colleagues that I have had the pleasure to work with over the years: Padraig Kennan and Ron Elsdon (University College Dublin) had a profound influence on my development as a geology teacher and researcher, particularly in the fields of Mineralogy, Crystallography and Igneous and Metamorphic Petrology. Paul Mohr, Paul Ryan and the late Andrew Brock (University of Galway) afforded me the opportunity to investigate the geological evolution of the Galway Batholith at PhD and postdoctoral level. The support and advice they gave me during those years of research was formative. I wish to acknowledge the many productive discussions I have had with Bernard Leake both as a PhD student and during his ongoing, annual research trips to Connemara.

To Stephen Whitmeyer and Eric Pyle (James Madison University, Virginia), the late David Gibson (University of Maine), Drew Coleman (University of North Carolina), the late Declan De Paor (Old Dominion University) and the staff of the College of William and Mary, Virginia for affording me the opportunity to teach the geology of Connemara to their undergraduate students. To Andrew Rankin (Imperial College London and Kingston University London, UK), David Selby (Durham University, UK), Derek Wilton (Memorial University, Newfoundland) and John Parnell (University of Aberdeen, Scotland) for their research support over the years.

To the late Ambrose Joyce and Ambrose Joyce Jr. for access to their Connemara Marble quarries for research and teaching purposes. To Marie Mannion (Heritage officer, Galway County Council) for her constant encouragement and support over the years. I am grateful to Andrew Smith for proofreading the text and his many constructive criticisms during the writing of this book.

About the Author

Martin Feely is an Emeritus Professor of Earth and Ocean Sciences in the School of Natural Sciences, University of Galway, Ireland, where he served as a teaching staff member from 1976 to 2014. He was Adjunct Professor of Geological and Environmental Sciences at James Madison University (JMU), Virginia, USA. His teaching experience included courses on crystallography, mineralogy, optical mineralogy, gemmology and petrology. He contributed annually to Boston University's (1997–2005) and JMU's (2006–2019) six-week geology field camp based in Connemara. He directed (1997–2017) a four-week annual geology summer school for The College of William and Mary, Virginia, USA. He established the University's Geofluids Research Laboratory in 1990. His research results on geofluid systems, in Ireland, the North Sea, Canada, South America, the United States, Africa, Tibet, China, the Middle East and Europe have been published in international geoscience journals. In 2004, he established the ongoing two-year Diploma in Scientific Studies (Gemmology) at the University of Galway. He has authored/co-authored over 200 scientific articles, papers and books and has presented his research at conferences throughout the United States, Canada and Europe.

1

Introduction to the Geology of Connemara

This chapter describes the regional geographical and geological setting of Connemara. The geology and the spatial distribution of Connemara's metamorphic and igneous rocks are outlined. The Connemara Metamorphic Complex (CMC) comprises two major rock groupings: the Dalradian metamorphosed sedimentary and igneous rocks and the younger Metagabbro Gneiss Suite. South of Clifden in western Connemara a semi-circular area some 5 km across occurs within the Metagabbro Gneiss Suite and is called the Delaney Dome. The rocks comprising the dome are early Ordovician metarhyolites exposed by erosion of the overlying rocks of the Metagabbro Gneiss Suite. The sub-horizontal contact between the two is a major thrust fault, the Mannin Thrust, which played a key role during the Grampian Orogeny in Connemara. The younger Galway Granite Complex (GGC) occurs to the south of the CGC and comprises a suite of minor plutons (~425 Ma), the Earlier Plutons and the younger Galway Batholith. The latter is composed of two plutons: the Carna (~410 Ma) and the Galway-Kilkieran (~400 Ma) plutons. The chapter concludes with an introduction to Connemara's glacial landforms, an intrinsic part of the region's world-renowned landscapes that play a key role in exposing the region's geological history.

Connemara: A Summary of Its Geographical Setting and Geology

Connemara is in the western part of County Galway and is an integral part of the Wild Atlantic Way. The region lies between the Atlantic Ocean in the west and the Corrib and Mask lakes of the Galway lowlands, in the east, and between Galway Bay in the south and Killary Fjord to the north (Figure 1.1).

DOI: 10.1201/9781032698410-1

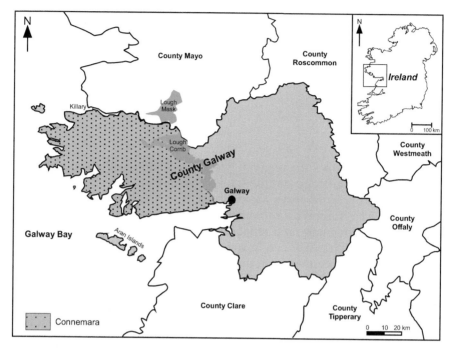

FIGURE 1.1
Map of County Galway showing the location of the Connemara region.

The latter forms part of the northern border between Counties Galway and Mayo. The name Connemara derives from the tribal name of an ancient maritime people known as the *Conmaícne Mara* (*mara* = 'of the sea'). Connemara is renowned for its geology, glaciated landscapes and biodiversity (Synge, 1979; Whilde, 1994; Leake and Tanner, 1994). The region covers an area of approximately 3000 km² (Figure 1.1).

The regional geology of Connemara is dominated by two major composite rock groupings: the Connemara Metamorphic Complex (CMC; ~700–462 Ma; Leake and Tanner, 1994; Friedrich and Hodges, 2016) and the younger Galway Granite Complex (GGC; ~425 to 380 Ma; Feely *et al.*, 2022) – Figure 1.2. The CMC comprises deformed and metamo phosed igneous and sedimentary rocks, the Oughterard Granite (~462 Ma; Friedrich *et al.*, 1999a, 1999b) and the Ordovician Delaney Dome (Leake and Singh, 1986) which is located south of Clifden. Ordovician and Silurian sedimentary and volcanic rocks (~500–410 Ma) are exposed to the north of the CMC (Dewey and Ryan, 1990, 2011; Graham *et al.*, 2022). The Ordovician South Connemara Group

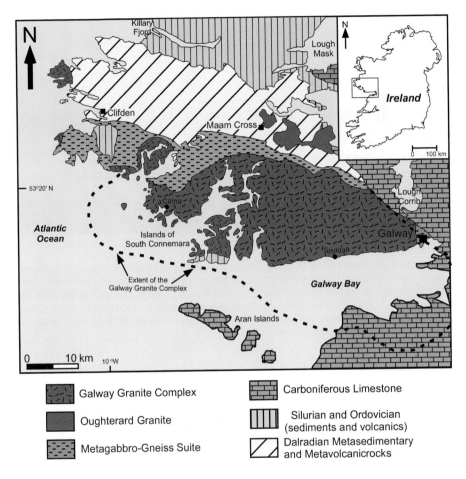

FIGURE 1.2
A simplified regional geology map of the Connemara area.

(Ryan and Dewey, 2022) is exposed, on the islands of south Connemara. The GGC extends under Galway Bay and the Carboniferous rocks of east County Galway (Murphy, 1952; Fairhead and Walker, 1977; Max *et al.*, 1983) – see Figure 1.2.

Connemara's landscape is dominated by the glaciated Twelve Bens and Maumturk mountains that form the Metamorphic Highlands of the Connemara Metamorphic Complex. In contrast, the lowland regions to the south are underlain by the Galway Granite Complex, i.e., the Granite Lowlands (Figure 1.3).

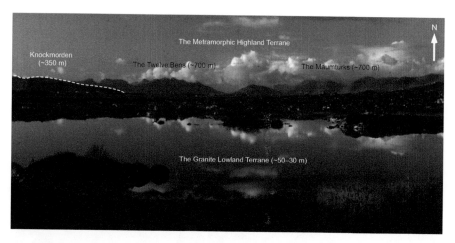

FIGURE 1.3

Connemara's Metamorphic and Granite Terranes. Note the significant change in topography from the Metamorphic Highlands (typified by the quartzite mountains of the Twelve Bens and Maumturks) in the north to the Granite Lowlands of the Galway Granite Complex (GGC). Knockmorden (~350 m) exposes the northern intrusive contact between the GGC and the rocks of the Connemara Metamorphic Complex. The granite terrane topography slopes southwards towards the northern shoreline of Galway Bay.

The Spatial Distribution of Connemara's Metamorphic and Igneous Rocks

The dominant bedrocks and the principal focus of this book are the rocks of the Connemara Metamorphic Complex (CMC) and the Galway Granite Complex (GGC). The CMC comprises the Dalradian metamorphosed sedimentary and igneous rocks and the Metagabbro Gneiss Suite. The GGC is a suite of granite plutons that are exposed along the northern coastline of Galway Bay (Figure 1.4). These two complexes extend from the Atlantic coast to the younger Carboniferous limestone strata of the east County Galway lowlands, where they are truncated by the Connemara Eastern Boundary Fault (Lees and Feely, 2016, 2017).

The geology of the two complexes is presented below.

The Connemara Metamorphic Complex

The Dalradian Metamorphosed Sedimentary and Igneous Rocks

These are Connemara's oldest rocks. They originated as sediments and basaltic intrusions, during the end of the Precambrian (Neoproterozoic)

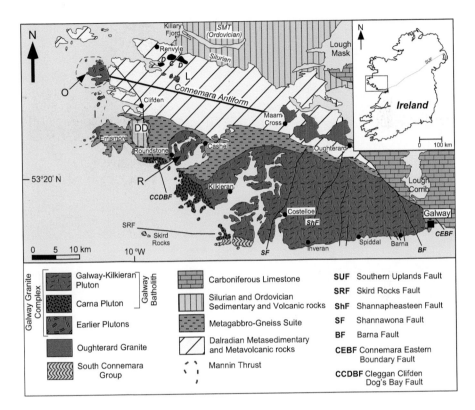

FIGURE 1.4

Detailed geologic map of Connemara. The dominant east-west trending metamorphic and igneous rock zones comprising the Connemara Metamorphic Complex (Dalradian metamorphosed sedimentary and igneous rocks and the Metagabbro Gneiss Suite) and the Galway Granite Complex are shown. The Earlier Plutons of the Galway Granite Complex are shown as follows: Roundstone (R), Inish(I), Omey (O) and Letterfrack (L) Plutons. The Ordovician rocks of the South Mayo Trough (SMT) are indicated. South of the Killary Fjord the Silurian Killary Harbour Formation lies unconformably on the Dalradian rocks. The Ordovician Metarhyolites of the Delaney Dome (DD) and its bounding Mannin Thrust are highlighted. The axis of the regional Connemara Antiform is shown. The Skird Rocks Fault (SRF) is the putative western extension of the Southern Uplands Fault (SUF) in Galway Bay see Leake (1978).

(Map adapted from Dewey and Ryan, 1990, 2011; Leake and Tanner, 1994; Pratch *et al.*, 2004; Graham *et al.*, 2022; Lees and Feely, 2016, 2017.)

and the early Cambrian (~750 and 550 Ma). They belong to the Dalradian Supergroup. The metamorphism and deformation of the Dalradian rocks occurred during the Grampian Orogeny (~472–462 Ma, Friedrich *et al.*, 1999a, 1999b; Friedrich and Hodges, 2016; Yardley and Cliff, 2022). Grampian age kilometric scaled folds are clearly visible in the landscape of the Connemara Metamorphic Highlands (Figure 1.5). The Dalradian is unconformably overlain along its northern margin by the Silurian Killary Harbour Formation. This formation occludes the contact between the Ordovician rocks of the

FIGURE 1.5
Kilometric scale folds visible on the southern facing slopes of the quartzite mountain, Letter-breckaun. A glacial corrie is also indicated. The foreground schists are covered by ~5000-year-old blanket peat bog with a cluster of cut and dried peat to the right, adjacent to the Inagh Valley road, heading north (R344; 53.531296°, −9.726266°).

South Mayo Trough and the Connemara Dalradian (Dewey and Ryan, 1990; Dewey and Ryan, 2011; Graham *et al.*, 2022; Badley *et al.*, 2023), (Figure 1.4).

The Metagabbro Gneiss Suite (MGGS)

Gabbros, quartz diorites and granites were intruded into the Connemara Dalradian rocks. Furthermore, they were deformed and metamorphosed, during intrusion, to form the Metagabbro Gneiss Suite at ~470–462 Ma, (Friedrich *et al.*, 1999a, 1999b; Friedrich and Hodges 2016; Downs-Rose and Leake, 2019; Yardley and Cliff, 2022). Differential weathering has led to a landscape typified by low-lying terrane extending south from the Oughterard-Clifden road (N59), interspersed with hills of metagabbros, e.g., Cashel Hill (Figure 1.6).

The northern boundary of the MGGS is marked by the incorporation of large rafts and blocks of Dalradian rocks that display various stages of assimilation in the metagabbros and granite gneisses. Partial melting of the Dalradian pelitic rocks has also occurred that produced migmatitic rocks (Leake, 1989). South of Clifden in western Connemara a semi-circular area some 5 km across occurs within MGGS called the Delaney Dome (Figures 1.4 and 1.7).

FIGURE 1.6
Cashel Hill metagabbro with the lower ground occupied by the paragneisses of the Metagabbro Gneiss Suite (Cashel Hill on R340; 53.432257°, −9.805393°).

FIGURE 1.7
The light grey-coloured fine-grained metarhyolites belong to the early Ordovician Delaney Dome Metarhyolite Formation (Leake, 2021) at Derrigimlagh, South of Clifden. The ice scoured Metamorphic Highland Terrane lies to the north (Lough Nagap, South of the R341; 53.457670°, −10.020743°).

The Delaney Dome comprises early Ordovician metarhyolites (Leake and Singh, 1986) exposed by erosion of the overlying rocks of the MGGS. The sub-horizontal contact between the two is a thrust fault, i.e., the Mannin Thrust, which was active during the Grampian Orogeny. The Dawros-Currywongaun-Doughruagh metagabbro intrusions (DCD; Figure 1.4) occur to the northwest and were intruded into the Dalradian rocks at ~472 Ma whereas the metagabbros of the MGGS were emplaced at ~470 Ma. (Friedrich *et al.*, 1999a, 1999b; Friedrich and Hodges, 2016; Leake 2021; Yardley and Cliff, 2022). In eastern Connemara the Dalradian rocks were intruded by the Oughterard Granite at ~462 Ma (Friedrich *et al.*, 1999a, 1999b; Friedrich and Hodges 2016; Yardley and Cliff 2022).

The Galway Granite Complex

The Galway Granite Complex (GGC) is a suite of granite plutons that are exposed along the northern coastline of Galway Bay, extending from Galway city in the east through the islands of south Connemara (e.g., Lettermore, Gorumna and Lettermullan) to Roundstone, and Omey Island, west of Clifden. The complex displays sharp intrusive contacts with the rocks of the Connemara Metamorphic Complex. The GGC comprises the four Earlier Plutons (Roundstone, Inish, Omey and Letterfrack Plutons), emplaced at ~423 Ma, and the Galway Batholith (comprising the Carna (~410 Ma) and Galway-Kilkieran (~400 Ma) Plutons). Leucogranite magma (Costelloe Murvey Granite) was emplaced at ~380 Ma into the Galway-Kilkieran Pluton (Feely *et al.*, 2003, 2007, 2010, 2018, 2022). Along the southern coastlines of Lettermullan and Gorumna Islands, the metamorphosed ocean-floor sediments and submarine lavas of the Ordovician South Connemara Group represent a fragment of the Iapetus Ocean floor, preserved as a roof pendant in the Galway Batholith (Fairhead and Walker, 1977; Ryan and Dewey, 2022), see Figure 1.2 and Figure 1.4.

Glacial Landscapes of Connemara

The Quaternary Period began ~2.6 Ma before the present when significant cooling of the Earth's climate occurred. It is divided into the Pleistocene (~2.6 Ma to ~11.7 ka) and the Holocene (~11.7 ka to the present day). The current climate represents an interglacial period, or a warm period between

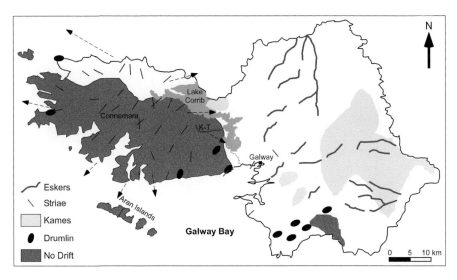

FIGURE 1.8

Map of County Galway showing the spatial distribution of the major glacial landforms (adapted from Synge, 1979). Note the general NE-SW alignment of the long axes of the drumlins and the eskers and shown by the directions of glacial striae on polished rock surfaces. The Killannin-Tullokyne esker (KT) just west of Lough Corrib is also indicated (Hennessy *et al.*, 2010; see Figure 1.10c). The Late Pleistocene ice-flow directions (black dashed arrows) in Connemara region are indicated (after Foreman *et al.*, 2022).

glacial advances. The glacial landscapes of Connemara (Mitchell and Ryan, 1997) are largely due to the last glaciation called the Midlandian (120,000–10,000 years before present). Foreman *et al.* (2022) reconstructed the timing and nature of the deglaciation of the Connemara ice centre. These authors report new cosmogenic ^{10}Beryllium (^{10}Be) ages from 15 glacial erratic boulders coupled with new geomorphic mapping. Their results indicate rapid widespread deglaciation of the last ice mass that occupied the Connemara region, at ~17 ka (Figures 1.8 and 1.9).

A site to the north of Moycullen (Figure 1.9a), i.e., Ballydotia (Baile Doite) area, is where Foreman *et al.* (2022) determined ^{10}Be ages of granite erratics ranging from 16,800 ± 300 yr. to 17,760 ± 410 yr., with mean and peak ages of 17.4 ± 0.6 ka and 17.7 ka respectively.

Patterns of deglaciation in Connemara are provided by the distribution of tills, gravels, sands and their associated landforms that formed during deposition and movement by the glaciers and their meltwaters, e.g., drumlins, eskers and kames. Much of west County Galway (i.e., Connemara) is devoid of glacial debris cover in stark contrast to the eastern part of the county where eskers are an integral part of the landscape. Drumlins,

FIGURE 1.9
(a) Carboniferous limestone pavement with erratics (E) of Connemara Basement (e.g., Galway Granite Complex). This location is in the Ballydotia (Baile Doite) area where Foreman *et al.* (2022) determined [10]Be ages of granite erratics. (b) Karst limestone pavement with vertical solution channels called grikes (a.k.a., grykes). The clints are the flat limestone areas cut by the grikes. Connemara Basement comprises the Connemara Metamorphic and Galway Granite Complexes (view looking west, Rocks Road, Moycullen; 53.362221°, −9.180095°).

however, occur in both western and eastern County Galway. Their long axis indicates the direction of ice movement, i.e., from NE to SW (Figures 1.8 and 1.10b).

Eskers are generally absent in Connemara but are common glacial landforms in eastern County Galway (Figure 1.8). The Killannin-Tullokyne esker is the best example of an esker in Connemara. It runs in an east-west direction for over 6 km from Tullokyne to Killannin. This esker, like many eskers in Ireland, was used by the local population to navigate their way through challenging areas of bogland and woodland (Figure 1.10c). Indeed, the Tullokyne to Killannin roadway runs along the top of this esker ridge.

In the west, the moving ice sheets left erosional landforms, e.g., U-shaped valleys, corries (cirques) and glacial striae. Noteworthy here is the Killary Fjord unique to north Connemara, where it defines the border between Counties Galway and Mayo (Figure 1.4).

The geology of the Connemara Metamorphic Complex is described in Chapters 2–5, and the geology of the Galway Granite Complex is presented in Chapters 6–9.

FIGURE 1.10

(a) Glacial valley (Lough Inagh Valley, R344) with corries on the SW facing slopes of the Maumturk Quartzite Mountains (elevation: ~600–700 m) (53.530337°, −9.724133°). (b) The Knock-Knockarasser-Gortgar drumlin swarm. Drumlin stoss and lee sides indicate that ice sheet moved from N to S. Easily recognisable as small asymmetric hills (~100 m in height), with verdant pastures, standing proud of the ~5000-year-old acid and peaty soils that typically cover the rocks of the Galway Batholith (view from the Knock River bridge on the L1320, looking to the NE; 53.283904°, −9.261999°). (c) The Killannin-Tullokyne esker, looking due west from Tullokyne (53.381241, −9.150458).

References

Badley, M.E., Graham, J.R. and Leake, B.E. 2023. Structural Control of the Deposition and Subsequent Deformation of the Killary Harbour-Joyce Country Silurian Succession. *Irish Journal of Earth Sciences*, 41, 1–26.

Dewey, J.F. and Ryan, P.D. 1990. The Ordovician Evolution of the South Mayo Trough, Western Ireland. *Tectonics*, 9(4), 887–901.

Dewey, J.F. and Ryan, P.D. 2011. Arc-Continent Collision in the Ordovician of Western Ireland: Stratigraphic, Structural and Metamorphic Evolution. In: Denis Brown and Paul D. Ryan (eds.) *Arc-Continent Collision*. Frontiers in Earth Sciences. Springer. 373–401. ISBN 978-3-540-88557-3.

Downs-Rose, K. and Leake, B.E. 2019. New Light on the Geology of the Roundstone Intrusion, Its Inversion and that of the Grampian Metagabbro-Gneiss Complex, Connemara, Western Ireland. *Irish Journal of Earth Sciences*, 37, 33–60.

Fairhead, J.D. and Walker, P. 1977. The Geological Interpretation of Gravity and Magnetic Surveys Over the Exposed Southern Margin of the Galway Granite, Ireland. *Geological Journal*, 12, 17–24.

Feely, M., Coleman, D., Baxter, S. and Miller, B. 2003. U-Pb Zircon Geochronology of the Galway Granite, Connemara, Ireland: Implications for the Timing of Late Caledonian Tectonic and Magmatic Events and for Correlations with Acadian Plutonism in New England. *Atlantic Geology*, 39, 175–84.

Feely, M., Gaynor, S., Venugopal, N., Hunt, J. and Coleman, D.S. 2018. New U-Pb Zircon Ages for the Inish Granite Pluton, Galway Granite Complex, Connemara, Western Ireland. *Irish Journal of Earth Sciences*, 36(1), 1–7.

Feely, M., McCarthy, W., Costanzo, A., Leake, B.E.L. and Yardley, B.W.D. 2022. The Late Silurian to Upper Devonian Galway Granite Complex. In: P.D. Ryan (ed.) *A Field Guide to the Geology of Western Ireland*. Springer Geology Field Guides. Springer Nature, Switzerland, 303–62.Print ISBN 978-3-030-97478-7.

Feely, M., Selby, D., Conliffe, J. and Judge, M. 2007. Re-Os Geochronology and Fluid Inclusion Microthermometry of Molybdenite Mineralisation in the Late-Caledonian Omey Granite, Western Ireland. *Applied Earth Science: Transactions of the Institution of Mining and Metallurgy: Section B*, 116(3), 143–49.

Feely, M., Selby, D., Hunt, J. and Conliffe, J. 2010. Long-Lived Granite-Related Molybdenite Mineralization at Connemara, Western Irish Caledonides. *Geological Magazine*, 147(6), 886–94.

Foreman, A.C., Bromley, G.R.M., Hall, B.L. and Jackson, M.S. 2022. A [10Be]-Dated Record of Glacial Retreat in Connemara, Ireland, Following the Last Glacial Maximum and Implications for Regional Climate. *Palaeogeography, Palaeoclimatology, Palaeoecology*, 592, article 110901.

Friedrich, A.M., Bowring, S.A., Martin, M.W. and Hodges, K.V. 1999a. Short-Lived Continental Magmatic Arc at Connemara, Western Irish Caledonides: Implications for the Age of the Grampian Orogeny. *Geology*, 27, 27–30.

Friedrich, A.M. and Hodges, K.V. 2016. Geological Significance of $^{40}Ar/^{39}Ar$ Mica Dates Across a Mid-Crustal Continental Plate Margin, Connemara (Grampian Orogeny, Irish Caledonides), and Implications for the Evolution of Lithospheric Collisions. *Canadian Journal of Earth Sciences*, 53, 1258–78.

Friedrich, A.M., Hodges, K.V., Bowring, S.A. and Martin, M. 1999b. Geochronological Constraints on the Magmatic, Metamorphic and Thermal Evolution of the Connemara Caledonides, Western Ireland. *Journal of Geological Society of London*, 156, 1217–30.

Graham, J.R., Dewey, J.F. and Ryan, P.D. 2022. The Silurian of North Galway and South Mayo. In: P.D. Ryan (ed.) *A Field Guide to the Geology of Western Ireland*. Springer Geology Field Guides. Springer Nature, Switzerland, 245–302. Print ISBN 978-3-030-97478-7.

Hennessy, R., Feely, M., Cunniffe, C. and Carlin, C. 2010. *Galway's Living Landscapes, Part 1: Eskers*. Published by Galway County Council, printed by Castle Print, Galway. 224p. ISBN 978-0-9567825-0-2.

Leake, B.E. 1978. Granite Emplacement: The Granites of Ireland and Their Origin. In: D.R. Bowes and B.E. Leake (eds.) *Crustal Evolution in Northwestern Britain and Adjacent Regions*. Geological Journal, Special Issue 10. Wiley, New Jersey, 221–48.

Leake, B.E. 1989. The Metagabbros, Orthogneisses and Paragneisses of the Connemara Complex, Western Ireland. *Journal of Geological Society of London*, 146, 574–96.

Leake, B.E. 2021. The Geology of the Clifden District, Connemara, CO. Galway, Ireland and Present Understanding of Connemara Geology. *Irish Journal of Earth Sciences*, 39, 1–28.

Leake, B.E. and Singh, D. 1986. The Delaney Dome Formation, Connemara, W. Ireland, and the Geochemical Distinction between Ortho-and Para-Quartzo Feldspathic Rocks. *Mineralogical Magazine*, 50, 205–15.

Leake, B.E. and Tanner, P.W.G. 1994. *The Geology of the Dalradian and Associated Rocks of Connemara, Western Ireland*. Royal Irish Academy. 96p. ISBN 1-874045-18-6.

Lees, A. and Feely, M. 2016. The Connemara Eastern Boundary Fault: A Review and Assessment Using New Evidence. *Irish Journal of Earth Sciences*, 34, 1–25.

Lees, A. and Feely, M. 2017. The Connemara Eastern Boundary Fault: A Correction. *Irish Journal of Earth Sciences*, 35, 55–56.

Max, M.D., Ryan, P.D. and Inamdar, D.D. 1983. A Magnetic Deep Structural Geology Interpretation of Ireland. *Tectonics*, 2, 431–51.

Mitchell, F. and Ryan, M. 1997. *Reading the Irish Landscape*. Publisher Town House. 392p. ISBN 186059055.

Murphy, T. 1952. Measurements of Gravity in Ireland: Gravity Survey of Central Ireland. *Dublin Institute for Advanced Studies, Geophysics Memoirs*, 2, Part 3, 31p.

Pracht, M., Lees, A., Leake, B., Feely, M., Long, B., Morris, J. and McConnell, B. 2004. *Geology of Galway Bay: A geological description to accompany the Bedrock Geology 1:100,000 Scale Map Series, Sheet 14, Galway Bay*. Geological Survey of Ireland. 76p.

Ryan, P.D. and Dewey, J.F. 2022. The South Connemara Group. In: P.D. Ryan (ed.) *A Field Guide to the Geology of Western Ireland*. Springer Geology Field Guides. Springer Nature, Switzerland, 229–44. Print ISBN 978-3-030-97478-7.

Synge, F.M. 1979. Quaternary Glaciation in Ireland. *Quaternary Newsletter*, 28, 10–18.

Whilde, T. 1994. *The Natural History of Connemara*. Immel Publishing Ltd. 336p. ISBN 0907151914.

Yardley, B.W.D. and Cliff, R.A. 2022. The Ordovician Arc Roots of Connemara. In: P.D. Ryan (ed.) *A Field Guide to the Geology of Western Ireland*. Springer Geology Field Guides. Springer Nature, Switzerland, 131–77. Print ISBN 978-3-030-97478-7.

2

The Connemara Metamorphic Complex: Dalradian Lithostratigraphy and the Metagabbro Gneiss Suite

The Dalradian is a mid-Neoproterozoic to early Ordovician sequence of largely metamorphosed clastic sedimentary rocks with horizons of metabasalts. The sediments were deposited on the southeastern continental margin of Laurentia. The oldest rocks belong to the Appin Group and were deposited in a shelf environment. Rocks of the younger Argyll and Southern Highland Groups formed in a series of fault bounded basins. The Dalradian rocks extend from Connemara through NW Mayo, the Ox Mountains, Donegal and then across to the Scottish Highlands. The Connemara Dalradian lithostratigraphy is divided into eleven formations: the Clifden, Connemara Marble and Barnanoraun Formations belong to the Lower Dalradian Appin Group; the Cleggan Boulder Bed, Bennabeola Quartzite, Streamstown Schist, Lakes Marble, Ballynakill Schist (includes Kylemore Schist and Cashel Schist Formations) and Cornamona Marble Formations belong to the Middle Dalradian Argyll Group; completing sequence is the Ben Levy and Lough Kilbride Formations that belong to the youngest Upper Dalradian Southern Highland Group. Each of these formations is described using field examples. Correlations between topography and geology are highlighted using digital terrain models. The Metagabbro Gneiss Suite provides outcrop scale examples of the syn-tectonic break-up of early consolidated gabbros by the later diorite and granite magmas. Amphibolites and a range of orthogneisses formed as result of these interactions. The metasediments (e.g., the Argyll Group's Cashel Schist Formation) marginal to, and occurring as xenoliths within the orthogneisses and metagabbros are hornfelsed and display varying degrees of partial melting leading to the formation of migmatites.

DOI: 10.1201/9781032698410-2

Introduction

The Connemara Metamorphic Complex (CMC) is comprised of two belts of metamorphic rocks called the northern belt and the southern belt (Figure 2.1). The northern belt is the widest and is mainly composed of Dalradian metasediments and metavolcanic rocks, e.g., pelitic and semipelitic schists and metabasalts (amphibolites). The southern belt has an interdigitational relationship with the Dalradian rocks of the northern belt. In stark contrast to the lithologies of the northern belt, the southern belt mainly consists of syn-tectonic metagabbros, orthogneisses and paragneisses, i.e., the Metagabbro Gneiss Suite (MGGS) (Figure 2.1). The orthogneisses are derived from dio-rites and granites intruded into the Dalradian rocks at ~468 Ma. The parag-neisses are derived from the Dalradian metasediments in proximity to the intruding metagabbros, diorites and granites.

The northern belt displays intricate kilometric scale fold patterns. They are displayed in particular by the marble horizons belonging to the Connemara Marble Formation. The standout feature of the regional map is the regional scale late asymmetric fold called the Connemara Antiform with a gently dipping (40–60° N) northern limb and a steep to vertical southern limb (Figure 2.1). It generally plunges eastwards at ~15–20°. The hinge zone is occupied by the Appin Group formations and the quartzites belonging to the Bennabeola Quartzite Formation in the area of the Twelve Bens (Figure 2.1). The Dalradian lithostratigraphy of the CMC's northern belt is described below followed by descriptions of the lithologies that comprise the MGGS of the southern belt.

The Dalradian Rocks of the Northern Belt: Plate Tectonic Perspectives

The Dalradian is a mid-Neoproterozoic to early Ordovician sequence of largely metamorphosed clastic sedimentary rocks with some horizons of metabasalts. Metamorphism and deformation of these sequences largely occurred during the Grampian Orogeny (~472–462 Ma). Sedimentation of the lower parts of the Dalradian Supergroup probably occurred ~730 million years ago in fault bounded rift basins within the supercontinent of Rodinia. Later sedimentation reflected increased crustal instability culminat-ing, between ~600 and 570 Ma, with major continental rifting leading to the birth of the Iapetus Ocean when the continents of Laurentia and Gondwana began drifting apart (Figure 2.2).

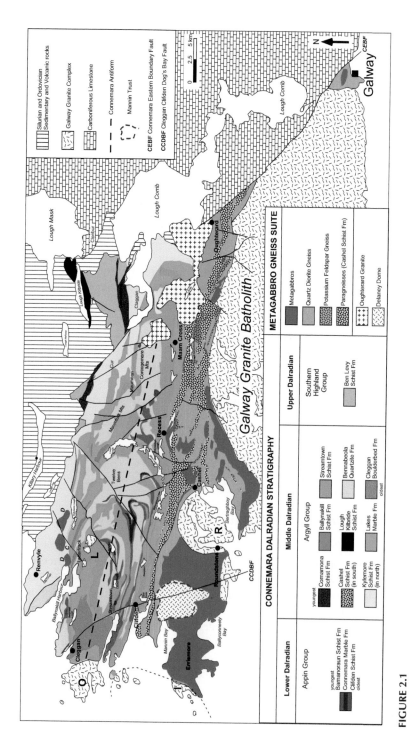

FIGURE 2.1

The geology of the Connemara Metamorphic Complex. The Dalradian metasedimentary and metavolcanic rocks of the northern belt contrast with the metagabbros, orthogneisses and paragneisses of the MGGS, i.e., the southern belt. The latter has an interdigitational contact with the Dalradian rocks of the northern belt. The axial trace of the Connemara Antiform is also shown. Note that the Cashel Schist Formation is part of the Argyll Group

(Continued)

FIGURE 2.1   (CONTINUED)

but is also included as part of the MGGS as the pelitic schists belonging to this formation were transformed into migmatites (paragneisses) during the intrusion of the ~470–468 Ma gabbros and granitic rocks into the Dalradian country rocks. The MGGS extends to the east of Galway city where the map indicates metagabbro and orthogneiss but may also include paragneisses (the area was originally mapped by Coats and Wilson, 1971 as migmatites). The slightly older ~472 Ma Dawros-Currywongaun-Doughruaigh (D-C-D) metagabbro occurs in the NW of the northern belt. The thrust contact (Mannin Thrust) between the Delaney Dome and the metagabbros is also shown. The CMC is bordered to the north by the Ordovician and Silurian rocks and to the east by the Carboniferous limestones. The granites of the Galway Granite Complex occur to the south, southeast and west, i.e., Early Plutons (~425 Ma) Omey (O), Inish (I), Roundstone (R) and Letterfrack (L) granites and the younger (~410–380 Ma) Galway Granite Batholith.

(Map adapted from Leake and Tanner, 1994; Feely *et al.*, 2010; Feely *et al.*, 2018; Feely *et al.*, 2020; Lees and Feely, 2016, 2017.)

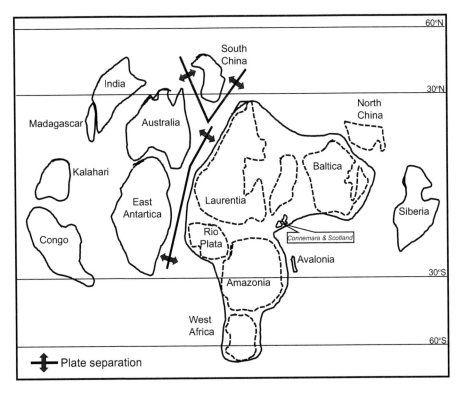

FIGURE 2.2

Breakup of the Rodinia supercontinent in a 750 Ma reconstruction. The location of Connemara and Scotland are indicated along with Avalonia.

(Adapted from Torsvik *et al.*, 2008.)

The Dalradian Lithostratigraphy

The establishment of the Dalradian stratigraphic sequences in Connemara is described in detail by Leake and Tanner (1994). A correlation exists between the Dalradian rocks of the CMC's northern belt and those exposed in NW Mayo, Donegal and the Central Highlands of Scotland. They were deposited on the southeastern continental margin of Laurentia. The older Dalradian rocks of Connemara (Appin Group) were deposited in a shelf environment and the younger Argyll and Southern Highland Groups formed in a series of fault bounded basins. Dalradian sedimentation occurred from Neoproterozoic to the early Palaeozoic (~700–520 Ma) with deformation and metamorphism mainly associated with the Grampian Orogeny (472–462 Ma). The Dalradian (called after the Celtic tribe, Dal Riada) is a tectono-stratigraphic term with nomenclatures rooted in the Scottish Highlands. The Grampian Terrane map (Figure 2.3)

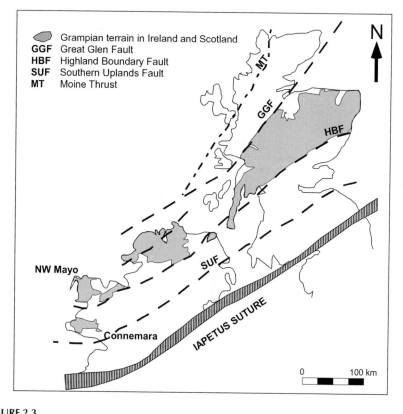

FIGURE 2.3

Grampian Terrane map showing the extent of the Dalradian Supergroup exposures in Scotland and Ireland.

(Adapted from Stephenson *et al.*, 2013.)

TABLE 2.1

Dalradian Stratigraphy of Connemara and a Brief Outline of the Lithologies Present in Each Formation. Formation thicknesses are indicative only

Dalradian Group	Formations	Lithologies
Southern Highland Gp. (~600–520 Ma) (Upper Dalradian)	Ben Levy Grit Fm. (1000–2000 m) and Lough Kilbride Schist Fm.	Gritty psammites and semipelites with pebbly horizons
Argyll Gp. (~625–600 Ma) (Middle Dalradian)	Cornamona Marble Fm. (<200 m)	Graphitic pelite, semi-pelite and marble
	Ballynakill Schist Fm. (<800 m)	Pelites & psammites; includes Kylemore Schist Fm. & Cashel Schist Fm. (in the S)
	Lakes Marble Fm. (<200 m)	Grey calcite marble, quartzite, pelite and amphibolite
	Streamstown Schist Fm. (<500 m)	Grey to brown psammite, semipelite and minor pelite. Amphibolite bands are common
	Bennabeola Quartzite Fm. (<1400 m)	White, grey and pink quartzite. Some amphibolite and pebbly horizons
	Cleggan Boulder Bed Fm. (<145 m)	Glacial tillite (granite and metamorphic clasts in a massive unstratified psammite)
Appin Gp. (~680–625 Ma) (Lower Dalradian)	Barnanoraun Schist Fm. (<130 m)	Rusty brown pelite and psammite. A m-thick dolomitic marble is at top of formation
	Connemara Marble Fm. (<80 m)	Green to grey and white coloured rock with serpentine, diopside, calcite and dolomite; amphibolite bands
	Clifden Schist Fm. (<50 m)	Pelite and semipelite

Source: Adapted from Leake and Tanner, 1994.

shows the Dalradian Supergroup extending from Connemara through NW Mayo, the Ox Mountains, Donegal and then across to the Scottish Highlands (Stephenson *et al.*, 2013). The Dalradian lithostratigraphy of the Connemara Dalradian rocks is tabulated in Table 2.1.

Summary descriptions of each formation are presented below.

Clifden Schist Formation

The rocks of the Clifden Schist Formation are the oldest strata exposed in Connemara. This formation consists of dark grey schists that are similar to those belonging to the Barnanoraun Schist Formation. Schists from both formations include dark grey schist with faserkiesel (millimetric scale, knots of interwoven fibres of the fibrous variety of sillimanite called fibrolite). According to Leake and Tanner (1994) and Leake (2021) it is not generally possible to separate them as mappable units. However, dark schist horizons stratigraphically below the Connemara Marble Formation are assigned to this formation. For example, in the Clifden area the schists are so tightly interfolded with the ones of the younger Barnanoraun Schist Formation that a clear distinction between the two has not yet been achieved (Leake, 2021). These formations are assigned the same colour on the regional map reflecting the uncertainty regarding their stratigraphic horizon (Figure 2.1).

Connemara Marble Formation

The presence of marble bedrocks belonging to the Connemara Marble Formation (and the younger Lakes Marble Formation) is recognised in the landscape by the green fields that carpet the marble bedrock. They contrast markedly with the typical peaty and acid soils overlying the other metamorphic rock types, e.g., quartzites and schists, of the Connemara Dalradian sequences (Figure 2.4).

FIGURE 2.4
View of Lissoughter Hill with a SW facing slope carpeted by green fields that overlie marble bedrock belonging to the Connemara Marble Formation. In the foreground, the peat bogs (~5000 years old) and peaty acid soils overlie the rocks belonging to the Streamstown Schist Formation (R344; 53.477357°, −9.724847°).

FIGURE 2.5
Lough Derryclare shoreline exposures of marbles belonging to the Connemara Marble Formation. Note the decayed or weathered condition of the marble outcrops typical of most marble exposures in this area (Lough Derryclare; 53.476246°, −9.752956°).

The Connemara Marble belongs to the Connemara Marble Formation. Heavily weathered marbles are typical of the exposures belonging to this formation (Figure 2.5). On closer inspection the pale whiter marble exposures display pseudomorphs of serpentine after tremolite (Figure 2.6).

The marble exhibits intricate millimetric to metric-scale corrugated layers whose colours range from white through sepias to various shades of green. The colour variations displayed by Connemara marble derive from the relative abundances of the coloured silicate minerals present (e.g., deep green hues appear when serpentine predominates). By contrast, white to grey marble such as that quarried at Carrara, Italy, consists of relatively pure calcite and/or dolomite-bearing marble. A small portion of the Connemara marble horizons contain sufficient proportions of carbonate minerals (calcite and dolomite) to be properly termed 'marble', and furthermore it is the other metamorphic minerals (e.g., olivine, diopside, clinochlore, chlorite and

FIGURE 2.6

Marble outcrop of the Connemara Marble Formation displaying green blades of serpentine pseudomorphs after tremolite set in a groundmass of calcite and dolomite (Lough Derryclare; 53.476246°, −9.752956°).

serpentine) that impart the colour varieties so typical of the stone traded as Connemara Marble (Figure 2.7).

Horizons of marble typically range up to 80 m thick. The marble is a metamorphic derivative of original impure siliceous dolomitic limestones. During the Grampian Orogeny new metamorphic silicate minerals formed, e.g., olivine, diopside, tremolite, talc and chlorite, whilst the original calcite and dolomite, locally representing significant portions of the rock, were recrystallised during metamorphism. Indeed, the relative proportions of all these minerals vary widely due to the different compositional layers present in the original limestone strata. Following initial high-grade metamorphism, hydrothermal metamorphism converted the earlier-formed minerals – olivine, diopside and tremolite – to serpentine (Figure 2.6).

The distribution of the Connemara Marble Formation within the folded Appin Group is depicted in Figure 2.8 (see also Figure 2.1). A very active Connemara marble extraction industry witnessed the establishment of

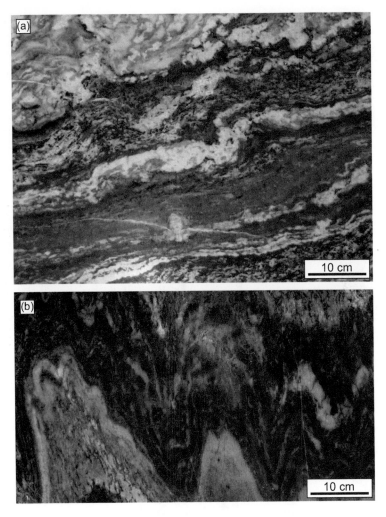

FIGURE 2.7
Polished slabs of Connemara Marble showing the typical polychromatic and folded layering. These are D3 folds formed at ~470 Ma. The greyish white bands in (a) reflect the predominance of the carbonate minerals, calcite and dolomite. The bands displaying deep green hues in (a) and particularly in (b) are due to an abundance of serpentine.

five main quarries located along the NW-SE axis of the Dalradian rocks (Figure 2.8) – see Feely (2002) for a detailed history of this industry.

Barnanoraun Schist Formation

The Barnanoraun Schist Formation consists of pelitic, semi-pelitic, psammitic and calcareous schists. These are best seen along the shoreline of Lough

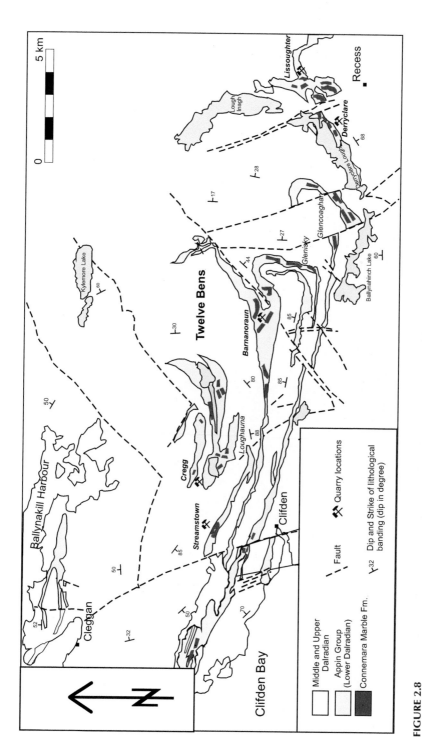

FIGURE 2.8

A simplified geological map showing the distribution of the Connemara Marble Formation within the Lower Dalradian Appin Group. The five main Connemara Marble quarry locations are: Streamstown, Cregg, Barnanoraun, Derryclare and Lissoughter. The folded nature of the Appin Group and the E-W distribution of the marble horizons reflect the presence of regional scale folds (see Chapter 3).

(Map adapted from Max, 1985.)

FIGURE 2.9
Ellipsoidal faserkiesel (knots of fibrolite) in Barnanoraun Schist Formation. The SW-NE fabric is the S3 schistosity (see Chapter 3). Loc.: shore of Lough Derryclare, 53.480677°, −9.746261°.

Derryclare where they occur in close proximity to marble horizons from the Connemara Marble Formation. Here the finely banded pelitic schists display aligned prominent knots of fibrolite (faserkiesel) that define the S3 schistosity (Chapter 3) (Figure 2.9).

The Cleggan Boulder Bed Formation

The Cleggan Boulder Bed Formation forms the base of the Argyll Group of the Middle Dalradian (Figures 2.1 and 2.10 and Table 2.1). This formation correlates with the Port Askaig Boulder Bed of Scotland. They are interpreted as subaqueous glacio-marine deposits of sand and cobbles (Figure 2.11). Both horizons formed during the Sturtian glaciation (~715–660 Ma) of the Cryogenian period (see Hoffman *et al.*, 2017). However, despite their stratigraphic position at the base of the Argyll Group there is uncertainty regarding the absolute age of both horizons.

The cobbles were stretched and flattened during the Grampian Orogeny. They commonly range up to 10 cm across, though some can reach 1 m across and include granite, quartzite and rare amphibolite. They are set in a matrix of grey schist, originally clay and sand. The formation is best seen on Cleggan Head, and on the southern slopes of Lackavrea near Maam Cross (Figure 2.11).

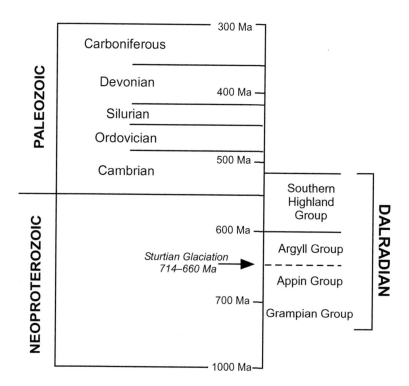

FIGURE 2.10
The Cleggan Boulder Bed Formation defines the base of the Argyll Group in Connemara. It is a correlative of the Port Askaig Boulder Bed Formation in Scotland. Their precise age is uncertain; however, both formed during the Sturtian glaciation (714–660 Ma). The broken line above reflects this uncertainty and is placed here at 660 Ma, indicating the minimum age of the glaciation.

Bennabeola Quartzite Formation

The Bennabeola Quartzite Formation (Figure 2.1; Tanner and Shackleton, 1979) consists of white to grey banded quartzites (band thicknesses range up to ~1 m). They form the E-W mountainous spine of Connemara typified by the Twelve Bens, the Maumturks and the Corcogemore Mountains (~600 to 700 m in height). These topographic highs reflect the resistant nature of the quartzites to weathering and erosion. Corries are a very common glacial erosion landform in these mountains (Figure 2.12)

The mineral content of the quartzite is ~80–90% quartz with minor feldspars (microcline and plagioclase) and micas (muscovite and biotite). Kilometric-scale folds are commonly observed on the quartzite mountain slopes and metric-scale folds are visible on many exposures (Figure 2.13). Occasional thin beds or lenses of pebbles are common towards the top part

FIGURE 2.11
Examples of cobblestones that occur in the Cleggan Boulder Bed Formation, exposed on the lower western slopes of Lackavrea Mountain, Maam Cross. (a) Fine grained grey quartzite; (b)–(d) are coarse-grained granite. The grey foliated quartz-rich matrix envelopes the cobbles. Note the folded nature of the matrix and cobble in (b) (R336, Lackavrea, Corcogemore Mountains; 53.491543°, −9.549130°).

of the formation. Heavy-mineral (e.g., magnetite and rutile) layers, some up to 10 cm thick, occur between the quartzite layers, e.g., at the western end of the Corcogemore Mountains. The topmost quartzite layers, where the Bennabeola Quartzite Formation passes up into the Streamstown Schist Formation, can display a dark grey colour due to the presence of graphite.

Streamstown Schist Formation

The Streamstown Schist Formation consists of laminated pelitic, semi-pelitic and psammitic schists (Figures 2.1 and 2.14). Amphibolite bands are common throughout the formation. Good exposures of schists belonging to the Streamstown Schist Fm occur along the N59 road between Recess and Clifden.

FIGURE 2.12
A view towards the NE of Letterbreckaun (left) and Knocknahillion (right) (Maumturk Mountain range) composed of the Bennabeola Quartzite Formation. Two ladle shaped depressions (corries) are also visible (R344, 53.52430°, −9.710964°).

The Lakes Marble Formation

The Lakes Marble Formation contains a wide range of lithologies that include blue grey marbles, quartzite, amphibolite, pelitic schists and calcsilicates. The marbles of this formation are essentially composed of calcite in contrast to the marbles encountered in the Connemara Marble Formation. Like the Connemara Marble Formation, green fields commonly overly marble bedrock (Figure 2.15). The calcite-rich nature of these marbles led to the construction of many lime kilns in marble areas, for example, on the north shore of Lough Derryclare. Adjacent peat bogs (~5000 years old) were used as a source of peat (turf) to fire the lime kiln (Figure 2.15).

Detailed mapping has established a sequence of four members (Lower Marble Member → Gritty Quartzite Member → Upper Marble Member → Banded Amphibolite Member) that are well exposed in the Cur Hill area (Figure 2.16). Here, the marble exposures display spectacular parasitic D3 folding (age = ~470 Ma) of grey-coloured marble layers with thinner black graphitic layers (see Chapter 3, Figure 3.10; Yardley and Long, 1983; Yardley and Cliff, 2022).

FIGURE 2.13
Folded bands of quartzite (~25 cm thick) belonging to the Bennabeola Quartzite Formation. These folds are ~470 Ma parasitic S folds (D3) (R344; 53.477044°, −9.742313°).

The Lakes Marble Formation hosts numerous late-19th- to early-20th- century base metal mines with concentrations of lead, zinc and copper sulphide ores especially in the Oughterard area, e.g., Glengowla mine where 19th-century extraction of ore occurred and its history is described in detail by Moreton (2019).

The Ballynakill Schist, Kylemore Schist and Cashel Schist Formations

The Ballynakill Schist Formation consists of dark brown to grey pelites and semi-pelites, quartzites and pebbly quartzites and massive amphibolites (Figure 2.1). Pelites with pebbly bands belonging to this formation are exposed on the slope of Cur Hill below the Lakes Marble Formation rocks. Here, schist exposures display fibrolite enveloping 2–3 mm garnets. These are in the upper part of the staurolite to sillimanite transition zone – see Chapter 4.

FIGURE 2.14
Typical exposure of laminated schists, Streamstown Schist Formation (R344; 53.466433°, −9.753328°).

FIGURE 2.15
A promontory of Lakes Marble Formation marbles with overlying green fields in contrast to the peaty acid soils developed on the quartzite bedrocks belonging to the Bennabeola Quartzite Formation. The location of an extant 19th-century lime kiln, built on the marble, is shown. This was used to manufacture lime (for fertiliser) from the calcite-rich marble. A view looking East of the NW shoreline of Lough Derryclare (53.473649°, −9.775766°).

FIGURE 2.16
Two members of the Lakes Marble Formation can be observed in the landscape along the R336, i.e., Upper Marble Member and the Banded Amphibolite Member. These are displaced by a NW-SE trending dextral fault which is probably part of the major Maam Valley Fault system. (Knocknagur (Cur Hill), Maam Valley, R344; 53.519111°, −9.609577°).

This formation is correlated with the Kylemore Schist Formation mapped by Badley (1976) and occurs north of Lough Inagh (Figure 2.1). Rocks of the Kylemore Schist Formation are exposed in the Claggan roadside quarry ~5.6 km to the east of Maam Bridge. Pinitised cordierite porphyroblasts (<3 cm across) are also present in pelites at the western end of the quarry (Figure 2.17).

The Cashel Schist Formation occurs along the southern limb of the Connemara Antiform (Figure 2.1). It consists of pelites, semi-pelites and psammites. These display augen structures and veins of quartzo-feldspathic material. The presence of Fe-rich pelites in the Cashel Schist Formation suitable for staurolite growth is a feature shared with the Ballynakill Schist Formation.

The Cornamona Marble Formation

The Cornamona Marble Formation is best seen in the Cornamona area at the western end of Lough Corrib (Figure 2.1). It consists of graphitic schists and graphitic marbles. Locally the marble is a calcite marble. According to Leake and Tanner (1994) there is an unequivocal upward transition from graphitic schist to a siliceous granoblastite of the Ben Levy Grit Formation north of Cornamona bridge. Serpentinite and talc schist lenses also occur near Cornamona and on Inishbofin. Leake and Tanner (1994) argue that these

FIGURE 2.17
Nebulous pinitised cordierite porphyroblasts (circled) in the Kylemore Shist Formation (Claggan roadside quarry; 53.496641°, −9.490985°).

lenses, also present in the Ben Levy Grit Formation, may have been emplaced later into their present locations in the solid state.

The Ben Levy Grit Formation

The Ben Levy Grit Formation consists of monotonous impure grey psammites and brown semi-pelites. The formation is largely restricted to the north side of Connemara (Figure 2.1). The Ben Levy Grit Formation contains ultramafic, serpentinite and metagabbro intrusions including those of the ~472 Ma. Dawros-Currywongaun-Doughruagh intrusions. The top of this formation is not seen as it lies under the unconformable Silurian rocks.

The Lough Kilbride Schist Formation

The Lough Kilbride Schist Formation is in faulted contact with the Ben Levy Grit Formation NE of Lough Kilbride (Figure 2.1). The psammitic and semi-pelitic schists are highly crushed and faulted. The metamorphic grade is high (sillimanite and cordierite schists and some migmatitic patches) in contrast to the lower-grade staurolite schists of the Ben Levy Grit Formation. According to Leake and Tanner (1994), it is unlikely that these rocks are younger than the Ben Levy Grit Formation as the metamorphic grade systematically decreases northwards until the faulted contact with the higher-grade Lough Kilbride Formation is encountered. The stratigraphical position of this formation is uncertain and cannot be conclusively shown to be older rather than younger, than the Ben Levy Grit Formation.

Geology and Topography Correlations

Visualisation techniques, in Connemara field geology research and education, were developed by geologists from the University of Galway, Boston University and the James Madison University (Hennessy and Feely, 2005; Hennessy and Feely, 2008; McCaffrey *et al.*, 2008; Whitmeyer *et al.*, 2009). For example, these include the development of virtual outcrop models of the folded marble horizons in the Connemara Marble Formation at Streamstown marble quarry and the iconic marble folds belonging to the Lakes Marble Formation at Cur. They were generated using terrestrial laser-scanning techniques and are accessible as short AVI (Audio Video Interleave) movies (McCaffrey *et al.*, 2008).

VRML (Virtual Reality Modelling Language) models have also been used to investigate the correlations between geology/stratigraphy and the glacially sculpted topography of the Twelve Bens area. Here, using VRML modelling, the geology of the Twelve Bens area (after Leake and Tanner, 1994) was draped over a digital elevation model (DEM) of the area by Hennessy and Feely (2005) (Figure 2.18). The model shows that in general the less resistant rocks belonging to the Connemara Marble Formation, Barnanoraun Schist Formation, Streamstown Schist Formation and Lakes Marble Formation form the floors of the valleys while the resistant quartzites of the Bennabeola Quartzite Formation (Figure 2.18).

The Southern Belt: The Metagabbro Gneiss Suite (MMGS)

The southern belt of the CMC comprises the metagabbros, orthogneisses and paragneisses that comprise the Metagabbro Gneiss Suite (MGGS) (Figure 2.1). The MGGS is mainly composed of metamorphosed gabbros and peridotites emplaced at ~470 Ma. These rocks were then intruded, enveloped and broken up by the emplacement of quartz diorite and granite magmas at ~468 Ma. Outcrop scale examples of the break-up of the early consolidated gabbro by the later granitic magmas are common (Figure 2.19).

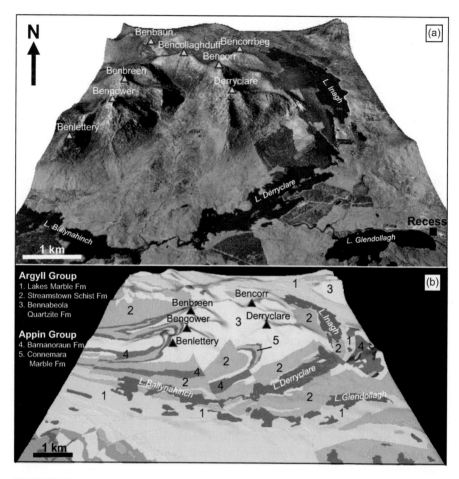

FIGURE 2.18

Aerial view and simplified geological map draped over the topography of the Twelve Bens area. The glacially sculpted mountains of the Twelve Bens, display numerous corries and glacial valleys. The mountains are formed of quartzites belonging to the Bennabeola Quartzite Fm. They contrast with the lowlands that are underlain by the softer and less resistant schists and marbles belonging to the Connemara Marble Formation, Barnanoraun Schist Formation, Streamstown Schist Formation and Lakes Marble Formation. (a) Digital Elevation Model (DEM) and (b) geological map of the area draped over the DEM highlighting the correlations between the bedrock geology and the glacially sculpted topography. The location of some of the individual bens is indicated, ranging in height from ~575 to ~730 m.

(Adapted from Hennessy and Feely, 2005.)

FIGURE 2.19
Dark grey-coloured xenoliths of metagabbro enveloped by the later granite orthogneiss. Examples of angular xenoliths are also highlighted. Scale is in centimetres (R341; Gowla river bridge, Cashel; 53.394765°, −9.776694°).

The granite magmas were metamorphosed to quartz diorite and granite gneisses collectively termed the orthogneisses. Marginal to and enclosed within the orthogneisses are partially melted (migmatitic) pelitic rocks belonging to The Cashel Schist Formation. These paragneisses form an integral part of the MGGS (Figure 2.1; also see Chapter 4). The belt strikes for 80 km east-west from Errismore in the west, to east-southeast of Oughterard. It then disappears into the later Galway Batholith and beneath the Carboniferous limestones, reappearing east of Galway city. A similar but smaller development of metagabbro and gneisses, the Dawros-Currywongaun-Doughruagh body, intruded into the Ben Levy Grit Formation of the northern belt. This body is slightly older (emplaced at ~472 Ma) than the gabbros of the southern belt (Yardley and Cliff, 2022) (Figure 2.1).

The Metagabbros

Two major gabbroic intrusions have been mapped in the southern belt: the large Errismore-Roundstone-Gowla intrusion in the south and southwest and the Cashel-Lough Wheelaun-Loughaunanny intrusion further east (Downs-Rose and Leake, 2019). The metagabbros range from peridotites (olivine- and pyroxene-rich rock) and pyroxenites (pyroxene–rich) to the predominant hornblende (±pyroxene), plagioclase bearing gabbros. Some preserve original igneous textures and minerals, e.g., olivine and pyroxene.

FIGURE 2.20
Cashel-Lough Wheelaun-Loughaunanny metagabbro displaying typical flat-lying igneous layering indicated by the dotted line (S. shoreline of Lough Wheelaun; 53.442843°, −9.744527°).

However, amphibolitisation has been widespread converting the gabbros to metagabbros also called amphibolites. Preserved igneous layering is a common feature displayed by outcrops of the metagabbro. For example, flat-lying metre scale layers, recognizable by grain size variations, are present near Lough Wheelaun in the Cashel-Lough Wheelaun-Loughaunanny intrusion (Figure 2.20).

Downs-Rose and Leake (2019) have shown that the Errismore-Roundstone-Gowla body and essentially all the Grampian metagabbro-gneiss complex from Slyne Head to Galway is inverted except for the Cashel-Lough Wheelaun-Loughaunanny intrusion and its envelope rocks.

The Ortho- and Paragneisses

The quartz diorite orthogneisses are mainly composed of quartz and plagioclase (andesine or labradorite) ± biotite, hornblende and potassium feldspar (Figure 2.21a). Orthogneisses with up to 60% potassium feldspar are called potassium feldspar gneisses (Figure 2.21b). They occur largely in the Cashel

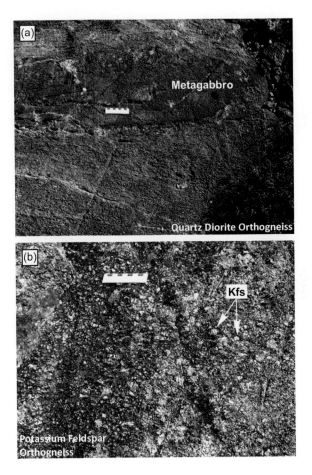

FIGURE 2.21
(a) Quartz Diorite Orthogneiss enveloping a dark grey lens of metagabbro (amphibolite) (Lough Aughawoolia, R336; 53.410142°, −9.540731°). (b) Potassium Feldspar Orthogneiss. The ~100° trending fabric is S3 and is apparent in both (a) and (b). Scale is in centimetres (~250 m South of Lough Nahasleam, R336; 53.432395°, −9.543986°). Abbreviations: Kfs: potassium feldspar.

area and are weakly foliated in comparison to the severely deformed quartz diorite orthogneisses (Figure 2.21).

The metasediments (e.g., Cashel Schist Formation) marginal to and occurring as xenoliths within the orthogneisses and metagabbros are hornfelsed and display varying degrees of partial melting to form migmatites. During partial melting the exsolved melt crystallised to form layers of quartz feldspar-rich leucosomes. They are interlayered with dark grey melanosomes the schistose part of the rock or restite where it has been depleted in granitic material during the partial melting. Unaffected schist is called the palaeosome. Superb exposures of migmatite occur near Lough Nahasleam (Figure 2.22).

FIGURE 2.22

Cashel Schist Formation migmatites display intricate patterns defined by granitic leucosome layers of quartz and feldspar that weather proud and contrast with the schistose melanosome layers. The schists are composed of biotite, quartz, plagioclase, potassium-feldspar, sillimanite and heavily altered cordierite. See Yardley and Warren (2021) and Yardley and Cliff (2022) (R336; west facing shoreline, ~200 m, west of Lough Nahasleam bridge; 53.436404°, −9.544915°).

References

Badley, M.E. 1976. Stratigraphy, Structure and Metamorphism of Dalradian Rocks of the Maumturk Mountains, Connemara, Ireland. *Journal of Geological Society of London*, 132, 509–20.

Coats, J.S. and Wilson, J.R. 1971. The Eastern End of the Galway Granite. *Mineralogical Magazine*, V38, 138–51.

Downs-Rose, K. and Leake, B.E. 2019. New Light on the Geology of the Roundstone Intrusion, Its Inversion and That of the Grampian Metagabbro-Gneiss Complex, Connemara, Western Ireland. *Irish Journal of Earth Sciences*, 37, 33–59.

Feely, M. 2002. *Galway in Stone: A Geological Walk in the Heart of Galway*. Published by Geoscapes. 48p. ISBN 0-9543412-0-1.

Feely, M., Costanzo, A., Gaynor, S.P., Selby, D. and McNulty, E. 2020. A Review of Molybdenite, and Fluorite Mineralisation in Caledonian Granite Basement, Western Ireland, Incorporating New Field and Fluid Inclusion Studies, and Re-Os and U-Pb Geochronology. *Lithos*, 354–355, 1–12.

Feely, M., Gaynor, S., Venugopal, N., Hunt J. and Coleman, D.S. 2018. New U-Pb Zircon Ages for the Inish Granite Pluton, Galway Granite Complex, Connemara, Western Ireland. *Irish Journal of Earth Sciences*, 36(1), 1–7.

Feely, M., Selby, D., Hunt, J. and Conliffe, J. 2010. Long-Lived Granite-Related Molybdenite Mineralization at Connemara, Western Irish Caledonides. *Geological Magazine*, 147(6), 886–94.

Hennessy, R. and Feely, M. 2005. *Galway County in Stone: The Geological Heritage of Connemara*. Series 1: Twelve Bens: Galway. Galway County Council and the Heritage Council.

Hennessy, R. and Feely, M. 2008. Visualization of Magmatic Emplacement Sequences and Radioelement Distribution Patterns in a Granite Batholith: An Innovative Approach Using Google Earth. In: D. De Paor (ed.) *Google Earth Science, Journal of the Virtual Explorer*. Electronic edn, vol. 29. paper 100.

Hoffman, P.F., Abbot, D.S., Ashkenazy, Y., Benn, D.I., Brocks, J.J., Cohen, P., Cox, G.M., Creveling, J.R., Donnadieu, Y., ...and Warren, S.G. 2017. Snowball Earth Climate Dynamics and Cryogenian Geology-Geobiology. *Science Advances*, 3, 11.

Leake, B.E. 2021. The Geology of the Clifden District, Connemara, Co. Galway, Ireland and Present Understanding of Connemara Geology. *Irish Journal of Earth Sciences*, 39, 1–28.

Leake, B.E. and Tanner, P.W.G. 1994. *The Geology of the Dalradian and Associated Rocks of Connemara, Western Ireland*. Royal Irish Academy. 96p. ISBN 1-874045-18-6.

Lees, A. and Feely, M. 2016. The Connemara Eastern Boundary Fault: A Review and Assessment Using New Evidence. *Irish Journal of Earth Sciences*, 34, 1–25.

Lees A. and Feely, M. 2017. The Connemara Eastern Boundary Fault: A Correction. *Irish Journal of Earth Sciences*, 35, 55–56.

Max, M.D. 1985. Connemara Marble and the Industry Based Upon It. *Geological Survey of Ireland Report Series*, 85(2), 1–32.

McCaffrey, K.J.W., Feely, M., Hennessy, R. and Thompson, J. 2008. Visualization of Folding in Marble Outcrops, Connemara, Western Ireland: An Application of Virtual Outcrop Technology. *Geosphere*, 4, 588–99.

Moreton, S. 2019. Glengowla: From Lead Mine to Show Mine. *Journal of the Mining Heritage Trust of Ireland*, 17, 3–14.

Stephenson, D., Mendum, J.R., Fettes, D.J. and Leslie, A.G. 2013. The Dalradian Rocks of Scotland: An Introduction. *Proceedings of the Geologists' Association*, 124(1–2), 3–82.

Tanner, P.W.G. and Shackleton, R.M. 1979. Structure and Stratigraphy of the Dalradian Rocks of the Bennabeola Area, Connemara, Eire. *Geological Society, London, Special Publications*, 8, 243–56.

Torsvik, T.H., Gaina, C. and Redfield, T.F. 2008. Antarctica and Global Paleogeography: From Rodinia, Through Gondwanaland and Pangea, to the Birth of the Southern Ocean and the Opening of Gateways. In: A.K. Cooper, P.J. Barrett, H. Stagg, B. Storey, E. Stump, W. Wise and the 10th ISAES editorial team (eds.) *Antarctica: A Keystone in a Changing World*. Proceedings of the 10th International Symposium on Antarctic Earth Sciences. The National Academies Press. 125–140. ISBN 978-0-309-11854-5.

Whitmeyer, S.J., Feely, M., De Paor, D., Hennessy, R., Whitmeyer, S., Nicoletti, J., Santangelo, B., Daniels, J. and Rivera, M. 2009. Visualization Techniques in Field Geology Education: A Case Study from Western Ireland. In: S.J. Whitmeyer, D.W. Mogk and E.J. Pyle (eds.) *Field Geology Education: Historical Perspectives and Modern Approaches*. Special Paper of the Geological Society of America, vol. 461. Geological Society of America, 105–15. ISBN 9780813724614.

Yardley, B.W.D. and Cliff, R.A. 2022. The Ordovician Arc Roots of Connemara. In: P.D. Ryan (ed.) *A Field Guide to the Geology of Western Ireland*. Springer Geology Field Guides. Springer Nature, Switzerland, 131–77. Print ISBN 978-3-030-97478-7.

Yardley, B.W.D. and Long, C.B. 1983. Eastern Connemara: Dalradian Metasediments and Associated Rocks. In: J.B. Archer and P.D. Ryan (eds.) Geological Survey of Ireland Guide Series No 4. Geological Survey of Ireland, Dublin, 62p.

Yardley, B.W.D. and Warren, C.E. 2021. *An Introduction to Metamorphic Petrology*. 2nd edn. Cambridge University Press. 333p.

3

Deformation History of the Connemara Metamorphic Complex

The rocks of the Connemara Metamorphic Complex record seven deformation phases (D1 to D7) that can be linked to folds, faults and fabrics. An additional deformation phase, D8, relates to the emplacement of the Galway Granite Complex which is the focus of Chapters (7 to 10) in this book. The deformation phases D1 to D7 and their structures are described with numerous field examples. D1 structures are not observed in the field, and their presence is based upon the interpretation of rare internal S1(?) fabrics in porphyroblastic garnets and feldspar. D2 is represented by a major isoclinal fold called the D2 Derryclare Fold that can be traced around numerous tight D3 folds. This D2 event is responsible for the earliest recognizable fabric, the S2 schistosity, developed in the CMC. The D3 folds are centimetric- to kilometric-scale folds. All metaigneous rocks belonging to the MGGS display regional-scale D3 folds. The dominant fold structure is the asymmetric D4 Connemara antiform that trends roughly SE-NW and plunges ~20° to the east. Its northern limb dips between 40° and 60° to the N and its southern limb has steep to vertical dips. The intersecting E-W Mannin Antiform (D5) and N-S Dolan Antiform (D6) formed the domal structure of the Delaney Dome. Late D6 brittle phase fault movements were widespread throughout Connemara between the end-Ordovician and early Silurian times. Major D7 E-W striking Scandian folding, at ~426 Ma, of the Silurian rocks occurs in north Connemara. These movements tightened the D4 Connemara Antiform making it a D4–D7 composite structure.

Introduction

The rocks of the Connemara Metamorphic Complex (CMC; Figure 3.1) record seven deformation phases (D1 to D7; Leake, 2021) that can be linked to folds, faults and fabrics (Figure 3.2). An additional deformation phase, D8, is included in the tabulation (Figure 3.2) but relates to the emplacement of the Galway Granite Complex, which is the focus of the later chapters (6–9) of this book.

DOI: 10.1201/9781032698410-3

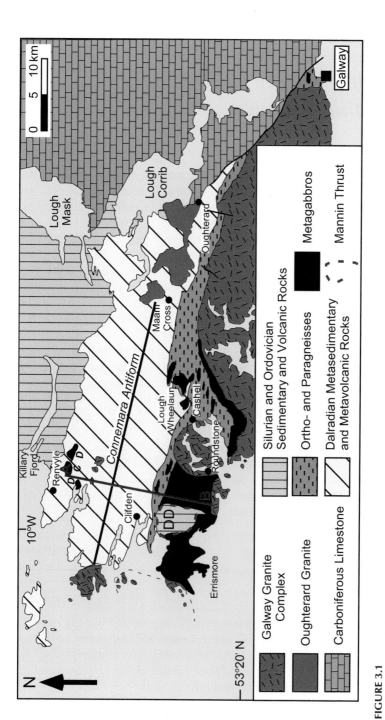

FIGURE 3.1

Geological map of the Connemara Metamorphic Complex (CMC) and its environs. The CMC is bounded to the north by Ordovician and Silurian sedimentary and volcanic rocks, to the south and west by the Siluro-Devonian granite plutons of the Galway Granite Complex. The eastern boundary is defined by a NW-SE trending faulted contact with the Carboniferous limestones. The metagabbros extend eastwards, for ~80 km, from the Errismore-Roundstone-Gowla Gabbro in the west through the Cashel-Lough Wheelaun-Loughaunanny Gabbro, to the eastside of Galway city. The Dawros-Currywongaun-Doughruagh Metagabbro intrusion (DCD) occurs to the northwest and was intruded at ~472 Ma whereas the metagabbros of the southern belt were intruded at ~470 Ma. (Friedrich and Hodges, 2016; Yardley and Cliff, 2022.) These metagabbros along with the ~468 Ma

(Continued)

FIGURE 3.1 (CONTINUED)
orthogneisses intruded the Dalradian Cashel Schist Formation triggering partial melting to form migmatitic paragneisses. These lithologies are collectively termed the Metagabbro Gneiss Suite (MGGS). The Oughterard Granite was emplaced at ~462 Ma. The lower Ordovician, Delaney Dome (DD) and the Mannin Thrust occur to the south of Clifden. Cross-section A-B is presented in Figure 3.4.

(Map adapted from Leake and Tanner, 1994; Leake, 2021.)

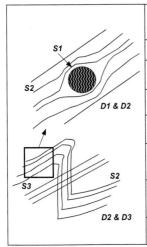

D1: Inclusion trails S1 in metamorphic minerals (porphyroblasts). *E.g.*: garnet. The porphyroblasts are enveloped by the later S2 schistosity. Rare and observed under the microscope.
D2: F2 folds with penetrative schistosity S2.
D3: F3 folds with S3 schistosity. Gneissic foliation in gneisses. The earlier F2 and their S2 are refolded by the F3 folds.
D4: Regional scale D4 Connemara Antiform, Joyces Antiform and the steep belt. The Oughterard Granite intruded the D4 Connemara Antiform at ~462Ma.
D5: Formation of the Delaney Dome: The Mannin thrust (454±4Ma) and the E-W D5 Mannin Antiform.
D6: Formation of the N-S Dolan Antiform and development of pairs of sinistral NE-SW and dextral NW-SE faults that opened a sedimentary basin into which the early Silurian sediments were deposited.
D7: Short-lived Scandian folding (~426Ma) of the Silurian and the CMC Tightening of the CMC's Connemara and Joyces D4 folds, and possibly the Mannin Antiform.
D8: Sinistral transpression to sinistral transtension accompanied by the emplacement of the Galway Granite Complex (~425–380Ma).

FIGURE 3.2
A tabulation of the CMC's deformation phases D1 to D7 after Badley (2014) and Leake (2021). D8 is included in the table. This facilitated the emplacement of the Galway Granite Complex, the focus of Chapters 6–8. Schematic (bottom left) showing a D2 fold refolded by D3, in a laminated pelitic schist. A sketch micrograph (top left) indicates the relationship between the schistosities S1, S2 and S3.

(Adapted from Wellings, 1998.)

The deformation phases (D1 to D7) and their structures are described under the following:

The Northern Belt.

The Southern Belt.

The Delaney Dome and the Mannin Thrust.

The Northern Belt

D1 structures are not observed in the field, and their presence is based upon the interpretation of rare internal S1(?) fabrics in porphyroblastic garnets and feldspar (see example in Friedrich and Hodges, 2016; p. 1262, Figure 3a). A schematic diagram outlining the relationship between the three schistosities, S1, S2 and S3, is presented in Figure 3.2.

In contrast, D2 is represented by a major isoclinal fold called the D2 Derryclare Fold that can be traced around numerous tight D3 folds, e.g., D3 the Glencoaghan Antiform (Figures 3.5–3.7). This D2 event was not preceded by any recognizable folds and is therefore responsible for the earliest fabric, the S2 schistosity, developed in the CMC. The D2 Derryclare Fold has the oldest sections of the Dalradian sequence, e.g., the Cleggan Boulder Bed Formation and the Connemara Marble Formation. The D3 folds are centimetric- to kilometric-scale folds that are recorded throughout the CMC. Most D3 fold axes plunge at <35° ESE and ENE. D2 and D3 folds are commonly coaxial, making it difficult at times to differentiate between S2 and S3 on the limbs of isoclinal D3 folds. Examples of S3 transecting S2, however, are readily observed in the hinge regions of D3 folds developed in the pelitic layers of laminated schists (Figure 3.3).

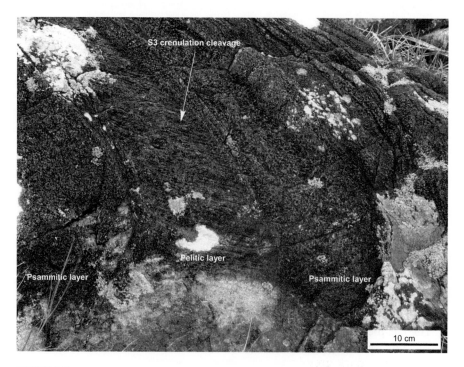

FIGURE 3.3
S3 crenulation cleavage in the hinge of a flat lying D3 fold. The S2 is clearly transected by S3 in the pelitic layers of this laminated (centimetric-scale psammite and pelite layers) schist, Streamstown Schist Fm. (junction of N59 with R344 ~1 km west of Recess; 53.466602°, −9.752514°).

The dominant fold structure of the Northern Belt is the asymmetric D4 Connemara antiform that trends roughly SE-NW and plunges ~20° to the east (Figures 3.1 and 3.4). The D4 Connemara antiform has a northern limb that dips between 40° and 60° to the N and a steep to vertical dipping southern limb. An E-W Steep Belt formally defined by Tanner and Shackleton (1979) is several kilometres across and has vertical foliation dipping 80–90° to north or south. This occurs 2–5 km to the south of the axial trace of the Connemara Antiform (Figure 3.5). The rocks of the Streamstown Schist and the Lakes Marble Formations commonly occur within this steep belt. D3 fold axes plunge at low to moderate angles to either west or east within the zone – it has been suggested that it is a root zone for D3 fold nappes (see Leake and Tanner, 1994, for a detailed discussion).

In the west, close to the Omey granite the D4 hinge zone is relatively narrow but broadens eastward towards the Twelve Bens. The form of the D4 antiform is outlined by the Bennabeola Quartzite Formation which trends eastwards, along the northern limb, from Cleggan through Diamond Hill to a broad area of outcrop in the Twelve Bens region and from there along the south limb westwards to Inishturk (Figure 2.1 in Chapter 2). Two D4 folds also occur in east Connemara, i.e., the Joyces Antiform and the Connemara Synform (Leake and Tanner, 1994; Leake, 2014).

The D3 Glencoaghan antiform can be observed from the N59 as it is well exposed in Glencoaghan on the southwesterly facing slope of Derryclare mountain (Figure 3.7). The D3 antiform refolds the D2 Derryclare fold. Furthermore, the Lower to Middle Dalradian stratigraphy, from the Connemara Marble Formation up through the Barnanoraun Schist Formation, the Cleggan Boulder Bed Formation to the Bennabeola Quartzite Formation, has been mapped in detail (Tanner, 1991; Leake and Tanner, 1994) (Figure 3.7).

On the southwesterly facing slopes of Letterbreckaun (Figure 3.8) kilometric-scale flat-lying D3 folds are displayed by the quartzites of the Bennabeola Quartzite Formation. To the east of Lough Derryclare by the Inagh Valley road, metre-scale asymmetric D3 folds occur in roadside outcrops of Bennabeola Quartzite Formation (Figure 3.8).

Near Clifden D3 folds in the Streamstown Connemara Marble Quarry are represented by the D3 Quarry and Crag antiforms (Figure 3.9). The hinge zone of the D3 Quarry Antiform, plunging ~25° west, was the target for extraction and quarrying of Connemara marble over the centuries.

The Upper Marble Member of the Lakes Marble Formation displays superb F3 folds (Figure 3.10). The grey marble bands with the interlayered, thin black to dark grey bands (graphitic) accentuate the F3 structures. An example of a refolded F2 is apparent in the upper-left corner of the exposure (also see image of this fold in figure 3D, p. 1262, in Friedrich and Hodges, 2016).

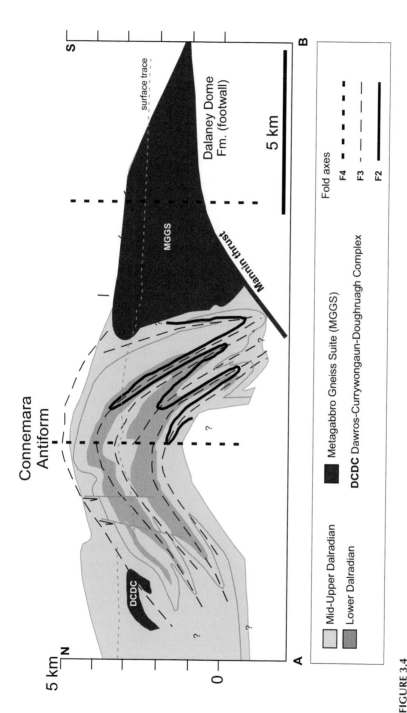

FIGURE 3.4
Simplified crossection (A-B; Figure 3.1) of the CMC highlighting the three fold phases associated with D2–D4. The amphibolite facies rocks of the Dalradian and the MGGS are thrust (by movement on the Mannin Thrust) over the greenschist facies rocks of the Delaney Dome Metarhyolite Formation. The DCDC is ~472 Ma, and the gabbros of the MGGS are ~470 Ma (Friedrich and Hodges 2016; Yardley and Cliff 2022).

(Adapted from Friedrich and Hodges, 2016.)

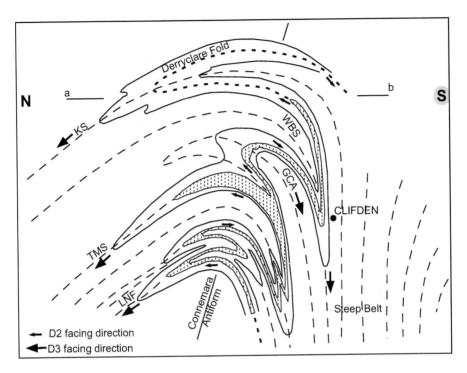

FIGURE 3.5
A schematic N-S structural profile across the D4 and D7 Connemara Antiform showing the steep northerly dip of its axial plane and the control exerted by the D2 Derryclare fold on the facing directions and folding directions of the major D3 folds. The core of the Derryclare fold is shaded reflecting the formations that are stratigraphically older than the uncoloured Bennabeola Quartzite Formation enclosed by D2 fold. All are folded around the D4 and D7 Connemara Antiform. Major D3 folds are KS (Knockpasheemore Synform), WBS (Waterloo Bridge Synform), GCA (Glencoaghan Antiform), TMS (Tully Mountain Synform) and LNF (Loch Nahillion Folds). Line a-b indicates present erosion level in the Maumturk Mountains and is ~10 km long. The locations of Clifden and the Steep Belt are shown.

(Adapted from Leake and Tanner, 1994; Leake, 2021.)

The Southern Belt

The Southern Belt (The MMGS) is described in detail by Leake (1986, 1989). The contact between the Dalradian sequences of the Northern Belt and the MGGS is relatively well-defined west of Cashel but becomes more variable further east. For example, at Cashel the contact is defined by the metagabbros against the Lakes Marble Formation while to the east isolated lenses of orthogneiss carrying metagabbro pods are interfingered with the Dalradian

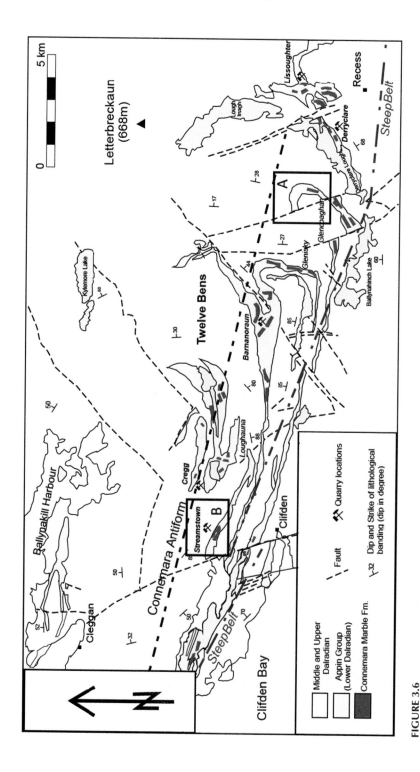

FIGURE 3.6

Simplified map showing the locations of Connemara Marble quarries and major D3 folds in the Twelve Bens area. The axial trace of the D4 Connemara Antiform is shown. Rectangular area A shows the location of the D3 Glencoaghan Antiform depicted in Figure 3.7. The southwesterly dipping slopes

(Continued)

FIGURE 3.6 (CONTINUED)

of Letterbreckaun (668 m), upper-right corner of map, display D3 folds that are depicted in Figure 3.8. Square area B shows the location of the Streamstown Connemara Marble quarry whose D3 folds are depicted in Figure 3.9. Note the change in dip across the D4 axis, i.e., the dip of the northern limb is ~50° N, whereas the southern limb is steep to vertical.

(Map adapted from Feely *et al.*, 2019.)

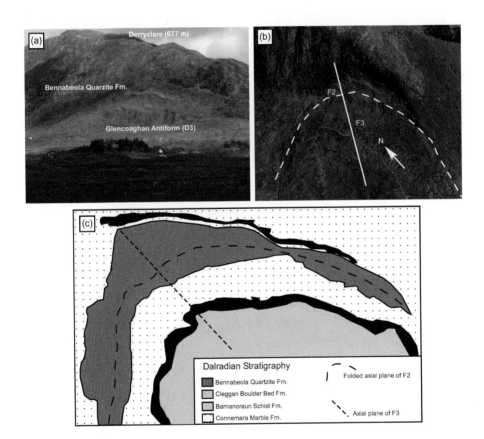

FIGURE 3.7

(a) The southwesterly facing slopes of Derryclare mountain expose the D3 Glencoaghan Antiform. It appears as a broad rounded hinge zone below a carapace of the Bennabeola Quartzite Fm. (b) An aerial view of Glencoaghan Antiform with the traces of the F2 refolded by F3 whose axial trace is shown. (c) The quartzite carapace encloses the older rocks comprising the Cleggan Boulder Bed Fm., the Barnanoraun Schist Fm. and the Connemara Marble Fm. The presence of the Connemara Marble Fm. in the core of the D3 antiform is reflected in the green grassy slopes of Glencoaghan.

(Adapted from Tanner, 1991 and Leake and Tanner, 1994 (Derryclare mountain; 53.486133°, −9.791733°).)

FIGURE 3.8
Kilometric-scale D3 folds on southwesterly facing slopes of Letterbreckaun (see Figure 3.6) (R344; 53.531590°, −9.724403°). These D3 folds are displayed by quartzites of the Bennabeola Quartzite Fm.

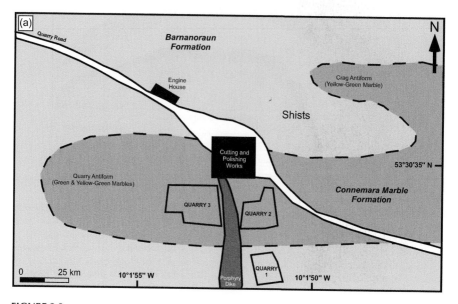

FIGURE 3.9
(a) Simplified geological map of the Streamstown Marble Quarry adapted from McCaffrey *et al.* (2008). The spatial distribution of the three quarries (1–3) is shown. Quarry 1 is the oldest (19th century) and Quarry 3 is the most recent. *(Continued)*

FIGURE 3.9   (CONTINUED)
(b) Quarry 3 shows the northern limb of the D3 Quarry Antiform which plunges at ~30° W. Marble bands dip ~55° N (east of the N59; 53.509898°, −10.032083°).

FIGURE 3.10
Upper Marble Member of the Lakes Marble Formation showing D3 folds and a refolded D2 fold (Knocknagur (Cur Hill); 53.519111°, −9.609577°). (*This is a strictly no hammer site and permission to visit must be sought from the landowner*).

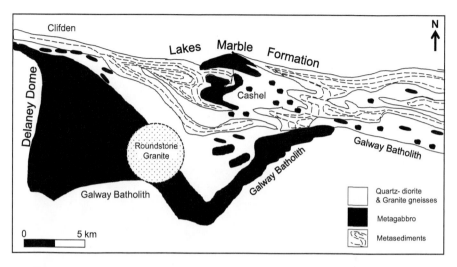

FIGURE 3.11

A simplified map of the western and central sectors of the contact between the Northern Belt's Dalradian metasediments and the MGGS. Note the kilometric-scale D3 fold structures displayed by the Cashel-Lough Wheelaun-Loughaunananny intrusion. The western edge is truncated by the Delaney Dome which is in thrust fault (Mannin Thrust) contact with the MGGS. The metasediments are mainly paragneisses belonging to the Cashel Schist Fm.

(Adapted from Leake and Tanner, 1994.)

metasediments (migmatitic in places, i.e., the paragneisses) (Figure 3.11). Indeed, rafts of metasedimentary rocks up to 200 m long occur within the Cashel-Lough Wheelaun-Loughaunanny intrusion (Figure 3.12). The syntectonic injection of the quartz-diorite and granite magmas (orthogneisses) into the metagabbros is apparent from the map (Figure 3.11). The orthogneisses disrupt and break up the metagabbros. All meta-igneous rocks display regional-scale D3 folds (Figure 3.11). The syntectonic envelopment of the Dalradian metasediments by the intruding magmas is common throughout the MGGS (Figure 3.11).

The metasediments, the orthogneisses and the metagabbros were all subjected to severe deformation during D3. The metagabbros acted as relatively rigid competent bodies and the D3 fabrics in the metasediments and gneisses are commonly deflected around the metagabbroic bodies. The orthogneisses commonly envelop torn-off fragments of the metagabbros and metasediments.

Detailed mapping combined with mineral and whole rock geochemistry by Downs-Rose and Leake (2019) reveal the inversion of the metagabbros, west of the Delaney Dome, and over the Dome and to the east in the Roundstone intrusion and still further east in Gowla. This demonstrates that the Errismore-Roundstone-Gowla body and practically all of the 80 × >20 km

FIGURE 3.12
A section of a 200 m long raft of laminated semi-pelites within the Cashel-Lough Wheelaun-Loughaunananny intrusion (Lough Wheelaun; 53.442843°, −9.744527°).

Grampian metagabbro-gneiss complex, from Errismore in the west to Galway in the east, is inverted except for the Cashel-Lough Wheelaun-Loughaunanny intrusion and its envelope (Figures 3.1 and 3.11).

The Delaney Dome and the Mannin Thrust

The Delaney Dome and the Mannin Thrust occur to the south of Clifden. The rocks of the Northern and Southern Belts tectonically overlie the metarhyolites of the Delaney Dome Formation. They are separated by the Mannin Thrust (Figures 3.13–3.15). A zircon U-Pb age of 474.6 ± 5.5 Ma (Draut and Clift, 2002) indicates that the Delaney Dome Metarhyolite Formation is a temporal equivalent of volcanic arc rocks (the Tourmakeady Volcanic Group) present in the adjacent South Mayo Trough. These were erupted during the Grampian collision of an oceanic island arc with the Laurentian margin. Furthermore, rare earth and high field strength element data show that the Delaney Dome Metarhyolite Formation and the Tourmakeady Volcanic Group are chemically similar and arc-like in character and suggests that the Delaney Dome Metarhyolite Formation is an along-strike equivalent of the Tourmakeady Group, strike-slip faulted south of the South Mayo Trough during or after the Grampian Orogeny (Draut and Clift, 2002). The metarhyolites of the Delaney Dome are an extrusive temporal equivalent of the metagabbro intrusions of the Southern Belt that penetrate the Connemara Dalradian meta-sediments. The Mannin Thrust was responsible for placing the whole of the high-grade (amphibolite facies) rocks of the CMC above the lower-grade rocks (greenschist facies) of the Delaney Dome Metarhyolite Formation (Leake *et al.*, 1983, Figures 3.13 and 3.14).

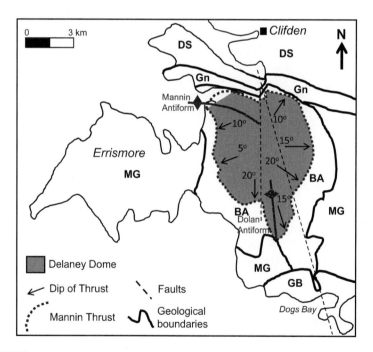

FIGURE 3.13

Geological map of the Delaney Dome derived from Leake and Singh (1986), Leake (2007), Leake and Tanner (1994), Downs-Rose and Leake (2019) and Leake (2021). The Delaney Dome is composed of the Delaney Dome Metarhyolite Fm. The Mannin Thrust is marked on the map between the Delaney Dome Metarhyolite Fm. and the Ballyconneely amphibolite (sheared ~470 Ma metagabbro) and dips outwards from the center of the Dome. Abbreviations DS: Dalradian schists; MG: Metagabbro; BA: Ballyconneely amphibolite; Gn: Gneisses; GB: Galway Batholith.

FIGURE 3.14
The Delaney Dome at Derrigimlagh, South of Clifden. Exposures of the Delaney Dome Metarhyolite Fm. are in the foreground. Moving northwards from here rocks of the Matagabbro Gneiss Suite are encountered followed by Dalradian sequences (Lakes Marble Fm., Streamstown Schist Fm. and the Bennabeola Quartzite Fm.). The topographic highs (e.g., Twelve Bens) are formed by the quartzites of the Bennabeola Quartzite Fm. Note the relatively low-lying topography of the Delaney Dome (~500 m south of R341; 53.457670°, −10.020743°).

FIGURE 3.15
Exposure of the severely deformed mylonitised metarhyolites belonging to the Delaney Dome Metarhyolite Formation. Scale is in centimetres (~500 m south of R341; 53.457670°, −10.020743°).

A ubiquitous SSE-NNW lineation on the Mannin Thrust plane indicates SSE-directed thrust movements (or indeed NNW-directed movements) took place above and below the line marking the thrust (Figure 3.13). Highly sheared and mylonitised lithologies occur above the thrust (the Ballyconneely amphibolite see Downs-Rose and Leake, 2019) and below lie the metarhyolites of the Delaney Dome Metarhyolite Formation (Figure 3.13–3.15). The domal structure of the Delaney Dome was formed due to folding of the Mannin Thrust zone and the rocks above and below it, by two intersecting broad open folds, i.e., the E-W Mannin Antiform and the later N-S Dolan Antiform assigned to the D5 and D6 stages respectively (Figure 3.13). Late D6 brittle phase fault movements were widespread throughout Connemara between the end-Ordovician and early Silurian times, i.e., ~443–438 Ma (Leake, 2021). Pairs of complementary sinistral NE-SW and dextral NW-SE faults dominate the regional geological map of Connemara. These faults opened a sedimentary basin into which the early Silurian sediments were deposited.

Geochronometry of the thrust-generated mylonitised Delaney Dome Metarhyolite Formation yields an age of 447 ± 4 Ma, i.e., Upper Ordovician (Tanner *et al.*, 1989). However, when this age is corrected for the newer Rb decay constant it becomes 454 ± 4 Ma (Leake, 2021). Leake (2021) argues that the thrusting cannot be D4 as posited by Friedrich and Hodges (2016) and Dewey and Ryan (2016). However, Friedrich *et al.* (1999a, 1999b) through precise U-Pb geochronology showed that the D4 had to be pre ~462 Ma, the age of emplacement of the Oughterard Granite that transects the D4 antiform. The age of the Mannin Thrust is ~454 ± 4 Ma and is assigned to D5. However, this Upper Ordovician age contradicts the D4 ~466–463 Ma age for the Mannin Thrust implicit in the plate tectonic model (Friedrich and Hodges, 2016) for the Grampian Orogeny in Connemara (see Chapter 5 for a detailed presentation and discussion of this model). The late Ordovician age (~454 ± 4 Ma) for the Mannin Thrust correlates with a 440–450 Ma late Grampian II event in Norway and Scotland (Downs-Rose and Leake, 2019; Leake, 2021). The deformation phases D1 to D7 and their structural elements are tabulated in Figure 3.2.

Leake (2021) proposes two more deformation events: D7 and D8. D7 relates to folding at ~426 Ma of Silurian rocks and tightening of D4 folds while D8 relates to major NW-SE and E-W faults and the intrusion of the ~425 to 380 Ma Galway Granite Complex.

References

Badley, M.E. 2014. The Connemara Antiform and Its Possible Silurian History. *Irish Journal of Earth Sciences*, 32, 71–8.

Dewey, J.F. and Ryan, P.D. 2016. Connemara: Its Position and Role in the Grampian Orogeny. *Canadian Journal of Earth Sciences*, 53, 1246–57.

Downs-Rose, K. and Leake, B.E. 2019. New Light on the Geology of the Roundstone Intrusion, Its Inversion and That of the Grampian Metagabbro-Gneiss Complex, Connemara, Western Ireland. *Irish Journal of Earth Sciences*, 37, 33–60.

Draut, A.E. and Clift, P.D. 2002. The Origin and Significance of the Delaney Dome Formation, Connemara, Ireland. *Journal of the Geological Society, London*, 159(2002) 95–103.

Feely, M., Wilton, D.H.W., Costanzo, A., Kollar, A.D., Goudie, J. and Joyce, A. 2019. Mineral Liberation Analysis (MLA)-Scanning Electron Microscopy (SEM) of Connemara Marble: New Mineral Distribution Maps of an Iconic Irish Gemstone. *The Journal of Gemmology*, 36, 456–66.

Friedrich, A.K., Hodges, K.V., Bowring, S.A. and Martin, M.W. 1999b. Geochronological Constraints on the Magmatic, Metamorphic and Thermal Evolution of the Connemara Caledonides, Western Ireland. *Journal of the Geological Society, London*, 156, 1217–30.

Friedrich, A.M., Bowring, S.A., Hodges, K.V. and Martin, M.W. 1999a. A Short-Lived Continental Magmatic Arc in Connemara, Western Irish Caledonides: Implications for the Age of the Grampian Orogeny. *Geology*, 27, 27–30.

Friedrich, A.M. and Hodges, K.V. 2016. Geological Significance of ^{40}Ar/^{39}Ar Mica Dates Across a Mid-Crustal Continental Plate Margin, Connemara (Grampian Orogeny, Irish Caledonides), and Implications for the Evolution of Lithospheric Collisions. *Canadian Journal of Earth Sciences*, 53, 1258–78.

Leake, B.E. 1986. The Geology of SW Connemara, Ireland: A Folded and Thrust Dalradian and Metagabbro Gneiss Complex. *Journal of Geological Society of London*, 143, 221–36.

Leake, B.E. 1989. The Metagabbros, Orthogneisses and Paragneisses of the Connemara Complex, Western Ireland. *Journal of Geological Society of London*, 146, 575–96.

Leake, B.E. 2007. The Geology of SW Connemara, Ireland: A Fold and Thrust Dalradian and Metagabbroic-Gneiss Complex. *Journal of the Geological Society*, 143(2), 221.

Leake, B.E. 2014. A New Map and Interpretation of the Geology of Part of Joyces Country, Counties Galway and Mayo. *Irish Journal of Earth Sciences*, 32, 1–20.

Leake, B.E. 2021. The Geology of the Clifden District, Connemara Co. Galway, Ireland, and Present Understanding of Connemara Geology. *Irish Journal of Earth Sciences*, 39, 1–28.

Leake, B.E. and Singh, D. 1986. The Delaney Dome Formation, Connemara, W. Ireland, and the Geochemical Distinction of Ortho- and Para-Quartzo Feldspathic Rocks. *Mineralogical Magazine*, 50, 205–15.

Leake, B.E. and Tanner, P.W.G. 1994. *The Geology of the Dalradian and Associated Rocks of Connemara, Western Ireland*. Royal Irish Academy. 96p. ISBN 1-8740445-18-6.

Leake, B.E., Tanner, P.W.G., Singh, D. and Halliday, A.N. 1983. Major Southward Thrusting of the Dalradian Rocks of Connemara, Western Ireland. *Nature*, 305, 210–13.

McCaffrey, K.J.W., Feely, M., Hennessy, R. and Thompson, J. 2008. Visualization of Folding in Marble Outcrops, Connemara, Western Ireland: An Application of Virtual Outcrop Technology. *Geosphere*, 4, 588–99.

Tanner, P.W.G. 1991. Metamorphic Fluid Flow. *Nature*, 352, 483–84.

Tanner, P.W.G., Dempster, T.J. and Dicken, A.P. 1989. Time of Docking of the Connemara Terrane with the Delaney Dome Formation, Western Ireland. *Journal of the Geological Society, London*, 146, 389–92.

Tanner, P.W.G. and Shackleton, R.M. 1979. Structure and Stratigraphy of the Dalradian Rocks of the Bennabeola Area, Connemara, Eire. In: Harris, A.L., Holland, C.H. and Leake, B.E. (eds.) *The Caledonides of the British Isles-Reviewed*. Scottish Academic Press, 243–56.

Wellings, S.A. 1998. Timing of Deformation Associated with the Syn-Tectonic Dawros-Currywongaun-Doughruagh Complex, NW Connemara, Western Ireland. *Journal of the Geological Society, London*, 155(1), 25–37.

Yardley, B.W.D. and Cliff, R.A. 2022. The Ordovician Arc Roots of Connemara. In: P.D. Ryan (ed.) *A Field Guide to the Geology of Western Ireland*. Springer Geology Field Guides. Springer Nature Switzerald, 131–77. Print ISBN 978-3-030-97478-7.

4

Metamorphism of the Connemara Dalradian and the Metagabbro Gneiss Suite

Pelitic rocks have played a key role in establishing the metamorphic history of the CMC. Amphibolite facies metamorphism is dominant throughout the region and the metamorphic grade increases southwards across a series of five E-W metamorphic zones. The lowest grade is the garnet zone, followed by the staurolite zone, the staurolite-sillimanite-transition zone, the sillimanite-potassium-feldspar zone and finally to the highest-grade zone, the migmatite zone, developed close to and within the MGGS. Early garnet-staurolite ± kyanite regional metamorphism (M2 Barrovian metamorphism) essentially related to D2 is overprinted by a syn-D3 sillimanite-grade metamorphic event (M3) in the southern half of the CMC. It is linked to conductive heat from the magmatic intrusions of the MGGS. The growth of andalusite, cordierite and sillimanite (fibrolite) typical of Buchan-style metamorphism is related to these magmatic events. Barrovian metamorphism (M2) occurred at pressures of ~5–6 kb and temperatures between 650° and 750°C. The later Buchan metamorphism (M3) was linked to lowering of pressure (due to the uplift of the CMC) to ~3 kb and temperatures of ~650°. The fifth and highest-grade zone is the migmatite zone: here syntectonic partially melted pelites (i.e., migmatites) that have plagioclase (albite) + quartz leucosomes (trondhjemitic) that have intermingled with the refractory portions of the metasediments, i.e., melanosomes. The latter commonly contain fibrolite, cordierite (always pinitised) and garnet. M3 metamorphism of impure siliceous carbonates within the lower Dalradian Connemara Marble Formation triggered the growth of silicate minerals that include olivine, diopside, tremolite, talc and clinochlore. Pervasive hydrothermal metamorphism followed, leading to wholesale serpentinisation of the earlier high-grade olivine, diopside and tremolite.

DOI: 10.1201/9781032698410-4

Introduction

Despite the CMC's wide range of metamorphic rock types described in the previous chapters, e.g., metagabbros (amphibolites), ortho- and para-gneisses, pelites, quartzites and marbles, this chapter focuses, although not exclusively, on the metamorphic history recorded by the pelites of the Connemara Dalradian. Prior to metamorphism, the Dalradian rocks of Conne-mara were a thick succession of mudstones, sandstones, impure limestones and basaltic lavas. Of all the protolith types found in a typical sedimentary succession, one of the most instructive to use in tracing metamorphic pres-sures and/or temperatures are pelitic rocks. They occur throughout the Connemara Dalradian succession and have played a significant role in establishing the metamorphic history of the CMC. Indeed, most detailed metamorphic studies of the CMC focussed on the pelitic rocks (Badley, 1976; Ferguson and Harvey, 1978; Yardley *et al.*, 1980; Leake and Tanner, 1994; Yardley and Cliff, 2022).

Metamorphism of the Connemara Dalradian Pelites

During progressive metamorphism, pelites develop a wide range of key metamorphic minerals, called *index minerals*, that are used to map meta-morphic zones that reflect progressive changes in pressure and temperature in orogenic terranes, e.g., Grampian Orogeny. In chemical terms metamor-phic reactions in pelites involve a range of chemical components, e.g., SiO_2, Al_2O_3, FeO, MgO, K_2O and H_2O, that play a key role in the chemi-cal reactions which produce the key metamorphic index minerals. Barrow (1893, 1912) was first to map a systematic variation in the mineralogy of Dalradian pelites in the SE Scottish Highlands that he clearly linked to changing pressure and temperature conditions of metamorphism. This work was refined later by Tilley (1925), who extended the field studies to the southwest. These regional zonal sequences are referred to as Barrovian zones and are recorded in pelitic rocks all over the world including the Dalradian rocks of the CMC. The Barrovian zones, developed in the CMC during the regional metamorphic event M2, reflect medium pressures and temperatures of metamorphism.

A second type of regional metamorphism, called Buchan style, was first described from Dalradian pelitic rocks in the Buchan region of the Scottish Highlands (Read, 1923, 1952). This style developed in the CMC during M3. This style of metamorphism, in contrast to the Barrovian metamorphism,

TABLE 4.1

Tabulation of Metamorphic Grade, Metamorphic Rock Types and Metamorphic Mineral Assemblages, for Barrovian and Buchan Styles of Metamorphism

Rock Name (Metamorphic Grade)	Medium P/T Regional Metamorphism Barrovian Zones	Low P/High T Regional Metamorphism Buchan Zones
Slate (low grade)	**CHLORITE** + quartz + plagioclase + muscovite	**CHLORITE** + quartz + plagioclase + muscovite
Schist (low grade)	**BIOTITE** + quartz + plagioclase + muscovite + chlorite	**BIOTITE** + quartz + plagioclase + muscovite + chlorite
Schist (medium grade)	**GARNET** + quartz + plagioclase + biotite + muscovite	**GARNET** + quartz + plagioclase + biotite + muscovite
Schist (medium grade)	**STAUROLITE** + quartz + plagioclase + garnet + biotite + muscovite	**ANDALUSITE** + quartz + plagioclase + cordierite + biotite + muscovite
Schist/Gneiss (high grade)	**KYANITE** + quartz + plagioclase + garnet + biotite + muscovite	**SILLIMANITE** + quartz + plagioclase + k-feldspar + muscovite
Schist/Gneiss (high grade)	**SILLIMANITE** + quartz + plagioclase + garnet + biotite + muscovite	

Notes: The index minerals for each zone are highlighted in bold upper-case lettering. The blue zones belong to the greenschist facies, and the red zones belong to the amphibolite facies (see Figure 4.2). Note that the zonal sequences at lower grades are similar for both styles of metamorphism. The Barrovian Garnet, Staurolite and Kyanite Zones typify the Connemara M2 event, and the Buchan Andalusite and Sillimanite Zones typify the later M3 event in Connemara (Leake and Tanner, 1994; Yardley and Cliff, 2022).

reflects low-pressure and high-temperature conditions of metamorphism and is characterised at low grades by a similar zonal sequence to that of the Barrovian; however, at higher grades a different zonal sequence is produced in pelitic rocks. The zonal sequences can be related to metamorphic grade, rock type and metamorphic facies (Table 4.1, Figures 4.1 and 4.2).

The three aluminium silicate minerals occur in the Dalradian pelites of the CMC (Table 4.1). Andalusite implies low pressure; kyanite is typical of high pressure and sillimanite forms in pelites at high temperatures (Figure 4.1).

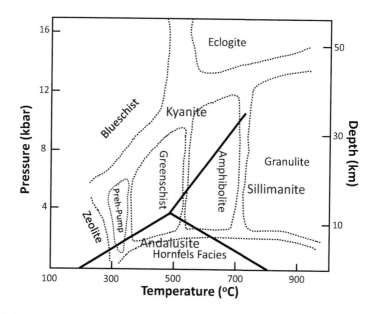

FIGURE 4.1

Pressure-temperature diagram showing the fields occupied by the various metamorphic facies. The approximate stability fields of the three Al_2SiO_5 polymorphs, andalusite, kyanite and sillimanite are also shown. Abbreviations: Preh-Pump: prehnite-pumpellyite facies.

(Adapted from Yardley, 1989. The Al-silicate phase boundaries are from Holdaway, 1971.)

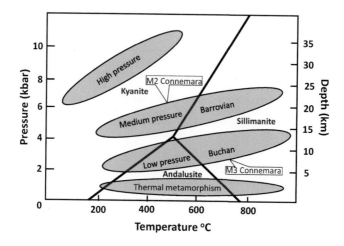

FIGURE 4.2

PT space showing the fields for the three main baric (pressure) types of metamorphism and the field for thermal metamorphism. Barrovian (medium-pressure M2) and Buchan (low-pressure M3) styles of metamorphism recorded in CMC are indicated. The stability fields for kyanite, andalusite and sillimanite are also shown.

(Adapted from Miyashiro, 1994.)

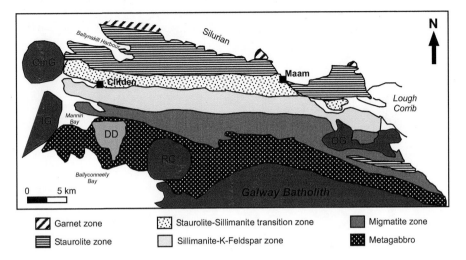

FIGURE 4.3
Metamorphic zones in the Connemara Metamorphic Complex. Abbreviations: OmG: Omey Granite; IG: Inish Granite; RG: Roundstone Granite; DD: Delaney Dome; OG: Oughterard Granite.

(Adapted from Yardley *et al.*, 1987.)

The amphibolite facies is dominant throughout the CMC, and the metamorphic grade increases southwards across a series of five E-W metamorphic zones (Figure 4.3). The zonal sequence is based upon the recognition of metamorphic index minerals in the Dalradian pelitic schists. The lowest-grade zone is the Barrovian garnet zone, followed in turn by the Barrovian staurolite zone, then the staurolite-sillimanite-transition zone, the sillimanite-potassium-feldspar zone and finally to the highest grade, the migmatite zone developed close to and within the MGGS.

The metamorphic history comprises an early garnet-staurolite ± kyanite (kyanite is very rare) regional metamorphism (M2 Barrovian metamorphism) essentially related to D2, which is overprinted by a syn-D3 thermal metamorphic event (M3) which is at sillimanite grade in the southern half of the CMC and is related to conductive heat from the magmatic intrusions of the synorogenic gabbros, quartz-diorites and granites of the MGGS. The growth of the index minerals andalusite, cordierite and sillimanite (fibrolite) typical of Buchan-style metamorphism is related to these magmatic events.

Barrovian metamorphism occurred at pressures of ~5–6 kb and temperatures between 650° and 750°C. The later Buchan metamorphism (M3) was linked to lowering of pressure (due to the uplift of the CMC) to ~3 kb and

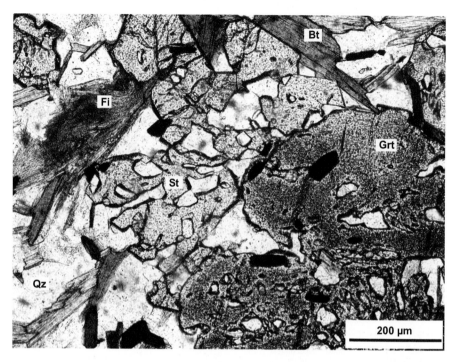

FIGURE 4.4
Photomicrograph in plane polarised light (PPL) of a pelitic schist belonging to the Ballynakill
Schist Fm. at Cur Hill (53.515437°, −9.610180°). The metamorphic index minerals belonging to
M2 (garnet and staurolite) and M3 (fibrolite) are shown. Abbreviations: biotite (Bt), quartz (Qz),
staurolite (St), garnet (Grt), fibrolite (Fi).

temperatures of ~650°. Pelitic schists belonging to the Ballynakill Schist
Formation (Figure 4.4) display the transition from M2 to M3 near Cur Hill.
Here the pelitic schist assemblage of garnet (M2) + staurolite (M2) + fibrolite
(M3) attest to this transition. Pinitised cordierites (M3) in pelitic schists belonging to the Kylemore Schist Fm are exposed at the Claggan roadside quarry
(Figure 4.5a). At this locality, the M2 staurolite zone schists of the Kylemore
Schist Fm are transected by M3 pegmatite veins that host centimetric-scale
pink andalusite + muscovite + quartz ± tourmaline (Figure 4.5b). This locality therefore contains metamorphic mineral assemblages that provide evidence of the M2 (staurolite + garnet) and the later M3 (cordierite+ andalusite)
metamorphic mineral assemblages. M3 faserkiesel are commonly displayed
by pelitic schists, Barnanoraun Schist Formation, near the shoreline of Lough
Derryclare (Figure 4.6a).

Mineral abbreviations used throughout this book are from Warr (2021).

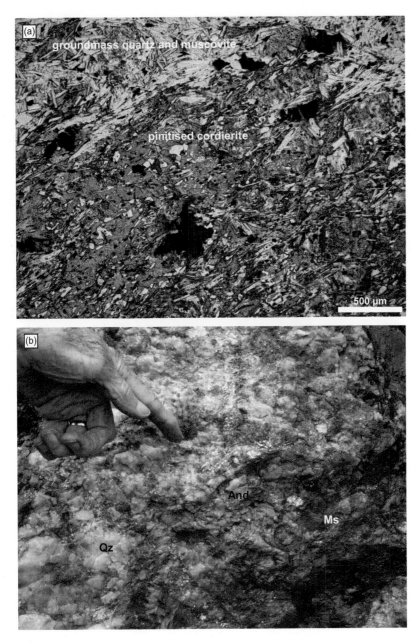

FIGURE 4.5
(a) Photomicrograph in PPL of a pelitic schist belonging to the Kylemore Schist Fm. displaying pinitised cordierite (M3) from Claggan roadside quarry (see Figure 2.17). (b) Pegmatite hosted pink andalusite (And), quartz (Qz) and muscovite (Ms) from the Claggan roadside quarry (53.496641°, −9.490985°). The pegmatites transect the schists of the Kylemore Schist Fm.

FIGURE 4.6

(a) M3 *Faserkiesel* (ellipsoidal concentrations of fibrous sillimanite called Fibrolite – Fi) in pelitic schist, Barnanoraun Schist Fm., Lough Derryclare (53.480677°, −9.746261°). (b) Migmatite, Cashel Schist Fm., Lough Nahasleam. The plagioclase + quartz (without potassium-feldspar) trondhjemitic leucosomes contrast with the darker brown-coloured melanosomes containing pinitised cordierite, fibrolite and locally red centimetric-scale garnets. The fabric trends ~E-W and defines the S3 (53.436368°, −9.544923°).

The Migmatites and Granulites of the MGGS

The fifth and highest-grade zone is the migmatite zone (Figure 4.3). Here syntectonic partially melted pelites (i.e., migmatites or paragneisses) belonging to the Cashel Schist Formation (Figure 4.6b) occur. The migmatites have plagioclase (albite) + quartz leucosomes (trondhjemitic) that have intimately mingled with the refractory portions of the metasediments, i.e., *melanosomes*. The latter commonly contain fibrolite, cordierite (always pinitised) and garnet. By comparing the bulk chemical composition of un-migmatised Cashel Schist Formation with their migmatised equivalents, Yardley and Barber (1991) calculated that there was approximately 20% partial melting of the pelites during H_2O-saturated melting. Furthermore, the melt produced, crystallised to form the trondhjemitic leucosomes composed of quartz and albite (Figure 4.6b). Yardley and Barber (1991) report that the melting involved the addition of water as well as heat from the contemporaneous intrusion of the quartz diorites and granites belonging to the MGGS.

Incipient partial melting occurs within the Streamstown Schist Formation. For example, an abandoned roadside quarry, near Lough Oorid, on the north-side of the N59 exposes pockets of weakly partially melted (migmatised) schists belonging to the Streamstown Schist Formation that contrast with exposures of schists unaffected by partial melting. Here the quartz rich pockets contain centimetric-scale crystals of waxy green pinitised cordierite (Figure 4.7).

Some xenoliths of schists enveloped by the metagabbros reached high-temperature granulite facies metamorphism. This is marked by the occurrence of corundum in buff-coloured pelitic xenoliths (commonly <30 cm long) within the Errismore-Roundstone-Gowla and Cashel-Lough Wheelaun gabbroic intrusions. Feely *et al.* (2017) report the presence of the deep blue-coloured gem variety of corundum (i.e., sapphire) in these xenoliths (Figure 4.8). The sapphire occurs in intimate association with the minerals magnetite (Fe_3O_4) and rutile (TiO_2). The incorporation during high temperature metamorphism

FIGURE 4.7
Centimetric-scale waxy green crystals of cordierite in weakly migmatised schists of the Stream-stown Schist Fm. These, like most cordierite in the CMC, are pinitised (Lough Oorid, roadside quarry north of N59; 53.456109°, −9.607089°).

FIGURE 4.8
Photomicrograph (PPL) of a granulite-grade sapphire-bearing pelitic xenolith within the Errismore-Roundstone-Gowla Gabbroic intrusion. The deep blue sapphire (Sa) occurs along with plagioclase feldspar (Pl) and rutile (Rut).

of iron (Fe) and titanium (Ti) from these two minerals, into the crystal lattice of corundum, imparts the blue colour to create the gem variety, sapphire.

The Connemara Marble Formation

The most notable rocks of the Connemara Metamorphic Complex are, without doubt, the marble horizons of the Connemara Marble Formation. The Connemara marble is a metamorphosed impure siliceous dolomitic limestone. M3 metamorphism of these impure siliceous carbonates triggered the growth of silicate minerals that included olivine, diopside, tremolite (Figure 4.9), talc and clinochlore. In addition, calcite and dolomite occur throughout, locally representing significant parts of the mineralogical assemblages. Indeed, the relative proportions of all these minerals can vary widely due to the different compositional layers that were present in the protoliths.

FIGURE 4.9
Marble exposures belonging to the Connemara Marble Fm., Lough Derryclare shoreline (53.479160°, −9.752764°). (a) Jade green serpentine (Srp) and networks of tremolite (Tr) blades. The latter are invariably pseudomorphed by serpentine. (b) Acicular tremolite displaying a radial growth pattern. Lough Derryclare shoreline (53.481026°, −9.747652°).

Pervasive hydrothermal metamorphism followed, leading to wholesale serpentinisation (Figure 4.10) of the earlier high-grade olivine, diopside and tremolite. The serpentinisation may have been linked, in part, to the generation of hydrothermal fluids during and after emplacement of the later Galway Granite Complex (O'Reilly *et al.*, 1997; Feely *et al.*, 2019).

The petrological term marble *sensu stricto* is a metamorphosed limestone dominantly composed of carbonate minerals, i.e., calcite and/or dolomite that form white to grey coloured marble, for example, the classic

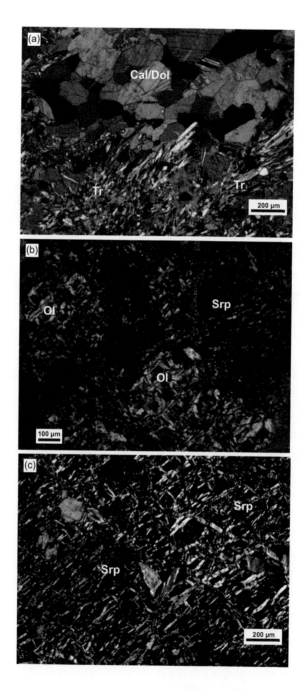

FIGURE 4.10
Photomicrographs (crossed polarised light, XPL) of marble belonging to the Connemara Marble Fm. (a) Millimetric-scale layer of calcite (Cal) and dolomite (Dol) with a lower layer relatively rich in tremolite (Tr). (b) Two pseudomorphs of serpentine (Srp) after olivine (Ol) set in a groundmass of serpentine. (c) Classic reticulated pattern displayed by serpentine which is also apparent in (b) (Streamstown Marble Quarry, 53.509898°, −10.032083°).

white Italian marble, Carrara Marble. Some horizons in the Connemara Marble Formation have a high enough proportion of carbonate minerals to be called *marble*; however, it is the other minerals (the silicates, e.g., serpentine, clinochlore, diopside) that give the unique colour varieties, sepia to jade green, so typical of the Connemara Marble. Mineral phase abundance data (Feely *et al.*, 2019) indicates that dolomite (14–59%), calcite (15–41%) and serpentine (15–35%) are the dominant minerals present across a range of samples. Less abundant mineral phases include diopside (0.30–12%), clinochlore (0.20–15%), phlogopite (0.40–7%), tremolite (1–8%) and omphacite (0.30–2%). The grey to white layers and patches are dominated by dolomite and calcite, whereas the green layers and patches reflect the presence of the silicates, serpentine and diopside. The centimetric-scale layers contain calcite and dolomite with diopside and serpentine. The diopside is spatially related to the serpentine reflecting the replacement of the former, along with other silicates, e.g., olivine (forsterite) and tremolite, during post-M3 hydrothermal metamorphism.

Metabasites

According to Leake and Tanner (1994) and Yardley and Cliff (2022), metabasites belonging to the Connemara Dalradian sequences are hornblende and plagioclase amphibolites. The meta-gabbro intrusions of the MGGS retain primary igneous layering and textures; however, the margins of these bodies have foliated amphibolites. Extensive data on the mineralogy and petrology of these rocks are presented in Leake (1989), and Leake and Tanner (1994). Recently, Downs-Rose and Leake (2019) presented the results of detailed geochemical and mineralogical studies of the Roundstone Intrusion and its structural setting within the regional MGGS. Downs-Rose and Leake (2019) reveal, for example, that the Roundstone Intrusion has six major components, the oldest being the Errisbeg Group whose mineralogy comprises: ortho- and clinopyroxenes + bytownite-anorthite that grade into bytownite-labradorite metagabbros. In the NW of Connemara, the rocks of the Dawros-Currywongaun-Doughruagh Complex (DCDC) preserve magmatic features much more clearly than the mafic rocks of the southern MGGS. This is due to the lack of later granitoid magmas within this area (Wellings, 1998).

Retrograde Metamorphism

Throughout the Connemara Metamorphic Complex retrogression of the high-grade metamorphic mineral assemblages in all rock types including

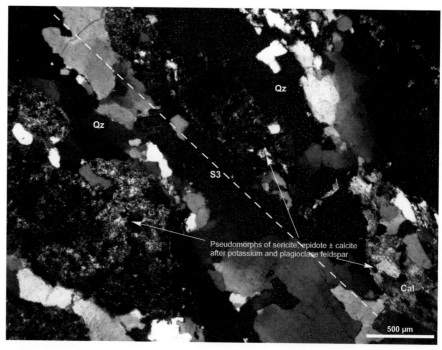

FIGURE 4.11
Photomicrograph (XPL) of orthogneiss from the MGGS displaying wholesale retrograde alteration of the feldspars to form pseudomorphs of fine-grained aggregates of epidote, sericite and
calcite. The D3 fabric (S3 striking at 120°) is delineated by dashed white line (~250 m South of
Lough Nahasleam, R336; 53.432395°, −9.543986°). Abbreviations: Qz: quartz; Cal: calcite.

the pelites, marbles and amphibolites is ubiquitous. For example, the marble
horizons in the Connemara Marble Formation display wholesale replacement of olivine, diopside and tremolite by the hydrothermal mineral,
serpentine (Figure 4.10). Elsewhere, hornblende, biotite and garnet are
replaced by chlorite, and the index minerals staurolite, andalusite, kyanite
and sillimanite are replaced by sericite. Cordierite is invariably pinitised
(Figure 4.5a). The orthogneisses commonly display intense retrograde
alteration of the feldspars replaced by aggregates of epidote, sericite and
calcite (Figure 4.11).

This retrogression and alteration of the earlier formed minerals is due
to fluxing of hydrothermal fluids through the Connemara Metamorphic
Complex and is linked, in part, to the later magmatic activities associated
with the assembly of the Galway Granite Complex (O'Reilly *et al.*, 1997;
Yardley and Cliff, 2022).

References

Badley, M.E. 1976, Stratigraphy, Structure and Metamorphism of Dalradian Rocks of the Maumturk Mountains, Connemara, Ireland. *Journal of the Geological Society, London*, 132, 509–20.

Barrow, G. 1893. On an Intrusion of Muscovite Biotite Gneiss in S.E. Highlands of Scotland and Its Accompany Metamorphism. *Quarterly Journal of the Geological Society, London*, 49, 330–58.

Barrow, G. 1912. On the Geology of Lower Deeside and the Southern Highland Border. *Proceedings of the Geologists' Association*, 23, 268–84.

Downs-Rose, K. and Leake, B.E. 2019. New Light on the Geology of the Roundstone Intrusion, Its Inversion and That of the Grampian Metagabbro-Gneiss Complex, Connemara, Western Ireland. *Irish Journal of Earth Sciences*, 37, 33–60.

Feely, M., Leake, B.E., Costanzo, A., Cassidy, P., Walsh, B. 2017. Sapphire Occurrences in Connemara: Field and Mineralogical Descriptions from an Erratic, and from Bedrock Pelitic Xenoliths in the Grampian Metagabbro-Gneiss Suite. *Irish Journal of Earth Sciences*, 35, 45–54.

Feely, M., Wilton, D.H., Costanzo, A., Kollar, A., Goudie, D.J., Joyce, A. 2019. Mineral Liberation Analysis (MLA)-Scanning Electron Microscopy (SEM) of Connemara Marble: New Mineral Distribution Maps of an Iconic Irish Gemstone. *The Journal of Gemmology*, 36(5), 456–66.

Ferguson, C.C. and Harvey, P.K. 1978. Thermally Overprinted Dalradian Rocks near Cleggan, Connemara, Western Ireland. *Proceedings of the Geologists' Association*, 90, 43–50.

Holdaway, M.J. 1971. Stability of Andalusite and the Aluminum Silicate Phase Diagram. *American Journal of Science*, 271, 97–132.

Leake, B.E. 1989. The Metagabbros, Orthogneisses and Paragneisses of the Connemara Complex. *Journal of the Geological Society, London*, 146, 575–96.

Leake, B.E. and Tanner, P.W.G. 1994. *The Geology of the Dalradian and Associated Rocks of Connemara, Western Ireland*. Royal Irish Academy. 96p. ISBN 1-8740445-18-6.

Miyashiro, A. 1994. *Metamorphic Petrology*. Oxford University Press. 404p. ISBN 0-85728-037-7.

O'Reilly, C., Jenkin, G.R.T., Feely, M., Alderton, D.H.M. and Fallick, A.E. 1997. A Fluid Inclusion and Stable Isotope Study of 200 Ma of Fluid Evolution in the Galway Granite, Connemara, Ireland. *Contributions to Mineralogy & Petrology*, 129, 120–42.

Read, H.H. 1923. The Geology of the Country Around Banff, Huntly and Turriff (Lower Banffshire and North-West Aberdeenshire). *Memoir of the Geological Survey, Scotland, Sheets 86 and 96 (Scotland)*. Her Majesty's Stationary Office, Nine Elms.

Read, H.H., 1952. Metamorphism and Migmatisation in the Ythan Valley, Aberdeenshire. *Transactions of the Edinburgh Geological Society*, 15, 265–79.

Tilley, C.C. 1925. Metamorphic Zones in the Southern Highlands of Scotland. *Quarterly Journal of the Geological Society, London*, 81, 100–12.

Warr, L.N. 2021. IMA-CNMNC Approved Mineral Symbols. *Mineralogical Magazine*, 85, 291–20.

Wellings, S.A. 1998. Timing of Deformation Associated with the Syn-Tectonic Dawros-Currywongaun-Doughruagh Complex, NW Connemara, Western Ireland. *Journal of the Geological Society, London,* 155(1), 25–37.

Yardley, B.W.D. 1989. *An Introduction to Metamorphic Petrology.* Longman Earth Science Series. 248p. Longman Scientific and Technical. Copublished in the US with J. Wiley and Sons, Inc., New York, ISBN 0-582-30096-7.

Yardley, B.W.D. and Barber, J.P. 1991. Melting Reactions in the Connemara Schists: The Role of Water Infiltration in the Formation of Amphibolite Facies Migmatites. *American Mineralogist,* 76, 848–56.

Yardley, B.W.D., Barber, J.P. and Gray, J.R. 1987. The Metamorphism of the Dalradian Rocks of Western Ireland and Its Relation to the Tectonic Setting. *Philosophical Transactions of the Royal Society of London,* A321, 243–70.

Yardley, B.W.D. and Cliff, R.A. 2022. The Ordovician Arc Roots of Connemara. In: P.D. Ryan (ed.) *A Field Guide to the Geology of Western Ireland.* Springer Geology Field Guides. Springer Nature, Switzerland, 131–77. Print ISBN 978-3-030-97478-7.

Yardley, B.W.D., Leake, B.E. and Farrow, C.M. 1980. The Metamorphism of Fe-Rich Pelites from Connemara, Western Ireland. *Journal of Petrology,* 21, 365–99.

5

Deformation, Magmatism and Metamorphism in the CMC: Pressure-Temperature-time (P-T-t) Perspectives

As the Iapetus Ocean floor was being subducted under the continents of Laurentia (carrying its then undisturbed and unmetamorphosed Dalradian sediments) and Avalonia, an intervening chain of offshore volcanic islands, including the Lough Nafooey Island, arc collided with Laurentia causing the Grampian Orogeny triggering the deformation, metamorphism and igneous intrusions that are recorded in the CMC. A series of schematic, time-related NW-SE cross-sections that track the formation of the CMC during the Grampian Orogeny form the core of this chapter. These are based upon field geology combined with mineral and rock chemistry and geochronology and track the deformation, metamorphic and magmatic histories of the CMC from ~472 to ~454 Ma. Several recently published PTt paths are combined to produce a composite PTt diagram for the CMC. The age of the Mannin thrust is addressed because movement on this structure played a key role in the assembly of the CMC. It occupies two points on the P-T-t path. The 466–463 Ma position on the path does not have supporting geochronometry. However, the geochronometry of the Mannin thrust mylonites provides a well-constrained late-Ordovician age (the D5 event ~454 ± 4 Ma), indicating that the thrust is a late Grampian D5 event.

Introduction

By the late Precambrian (~550 Ma), Amazonia, West Africa and Rio Plata had come together to create the super continent of Gondwana. The Iapetus Ocean had formed due to rifting between Baltica, Laurentia and Gondwana (Figure 5.1). The Iapetus Ocean then progressively widened until, during the Cambrian period, the process went into reverse.

DOI: 10.1201/9781032698410-5

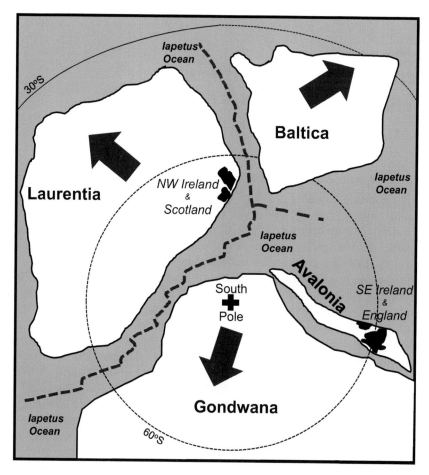

FIGURE 5.1

Precambrian map of the southern hemisphere at ~550 Ma showing the Iapetus Ocean with NW Ireland (including Connemara) and Scotland located on the continental edge of Laurentia. SE Ireland and England are part of Avalonia on the other side of the expanding Iapetus Ocean. Avalonia spalled off Gondwana. Arrows show the direction of plate movement and broken red lines indicate rifting.

(Adapted from Webster *et al.*, 2017.)

As subduction of the Iapetus Ocean floor under the continents of Laurentia (carrying its then undisturbed and unmetamorphosed Dalradian sediments) and Avalonia progressed, an intervening chain of offshore volcanic islands including the Lough Nafooey Island arc collided with Laurentia causing the Grampian Orogeny (Friedrich *et al.*, 1999a, 1999b; Friedrich and Hodges, 2016; Dewey and Ryan, 2016) (Figures 5.2a and b).

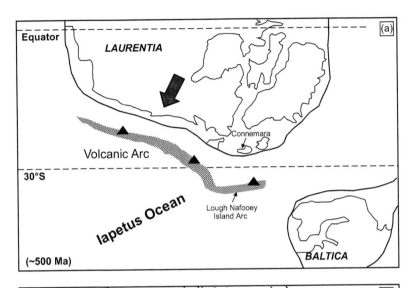

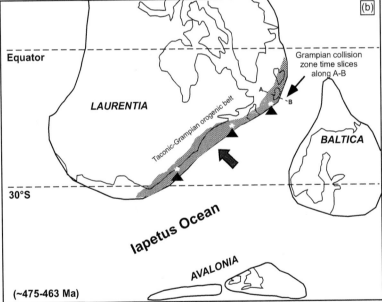

FIGURE 5.2

(a) Schematic showing plate distributions during late Cambrian. Southwesterly directed subduction of Laurentia under the Iapetan ocean crust created a volcanic arc that included the Lough Nafooey volcanic arc. (b) Schematic of the Early Ordovician collision between the volcanic arc (including the Lough Nafooey volcanic arc) and Laurentia creating the Grampian (Taconic in the US) Orogeny. Line A-B marks the position of the cross-sections that track the temporal progress of the Grampian Orogeny (Figures 5.3–5.6).

(Maps are adapted from Chew and Strachan, 2014.)

The Relative Timing of Deformation, Magmatism and Metamorphism in the CMC

Recent Recalculations of Previously Published Ages from the CMC

Yardley and Cliff (2022) present a new data set of recalculated ages using currently recommended values for decay constants. Previously published ages by Tanner *et al.* (1989), Cliff *et al.* (1993), Cliff *et al.* (1996), Friedrich (1998), Friedrich *et al.* (1999a, 1999b), Draut and Clift (2002) were recalculated and a detailed discussion on the significance of the new recalculated ages is presented by Yardley and Cliff (2022). The overall conclusion from the recalculated ages is that the arc-related magmatism and metamorphism in Connemara occurred between ~ 472 and 462 Ma and regional metamorphism in northern Connemara appears to have peaked at ~470 Ma. However, Yardley and Cliff (2022) advise caution when considering the regional significance of the CMC's geochronometry because: the number of dated samples remains small; the potential for Pb loss in the U-Pb zircon system leading to displacements to younger ages; the U-Pb single zircon data is not accompanied by petrographic and geochemical data on the individual dated grains; the presence of an inherited zircon component means concordant grains are rare.

A Series of Time-Related NW-SE Cross-Sections Tracking the Evolution of the CMC from ~472 to 462 Ma

A series of schematic, time-related NW-SE cross-sections that track the formation of the CMC during the Grampian Orogeny are presented in Figure 5.3 to Figure 5.6 (the line of section, A-B, is shown in Figure 5.2b). These are based upon field geology combined with mineral and rock chemistry and geochronology presented by Friedrich *et al.* (1999a, 1999b) and Friedrich and Hodges (2016), and the recalculated ages of Yardley and Cliff (2022) are used where appropriate.

By ~490 Ma, the Lough Nafooey Island arc had formed and the Laurentian continental margin and its Dalradian sedimentary and volcanic rocks were entering the subduction zone (Figure 5.3).

By ~472 Ma, the island arc, comprising (a) its forearc basin (the South Mayo Trough- Ryan *et al.*, 2022), (b) its frontal ophiolite complex (the Deer Park Complex exposed in Clew Bay-Daly *et al.*, 2022) and (c) the accretionary complex (Killadangan Complex, exposed in Clew Bay-Daly *et al.*, 2022; Ryan *et al.*, 2022), moved en masse northwards overriding the entire Dalradian strata. The Dalradian strata were thrust below the oceanic arc-mantle at the plate interface forming an orogenic wedge (Figure 5.4). During this time D2 and D3 structures developed and were linked to thrusting and collision-related compression. The resulting structural patterns in Figure 5.4 reflect the dominant kilometric-scale F2 and F3 folds that are readily observed in

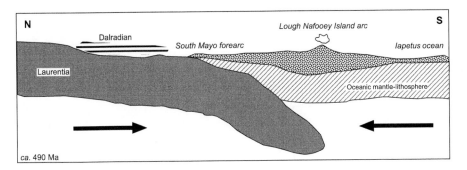

FIGURE 5.3
Schematic NW-SE cross-section showing the configuration of the Laurentian continental plate
and the Lough Nafooey Island arc. The Laurentian slab and its pile of undeformed Connemara
Dalradian strata were in the subduction zone at ~490 Ma when they were about to move under
the oceanic island-arc lithosphere. Black arrows indicate relative plate motion.

(Adapted from Friedrich and Hodges, 2016.)

the Connemara landscape and described earlier in Chapter 3 (e.g., at Glencoaghan and Letterbreckaun). The medium-pressure Barrovian-style metamorphism (M2) was essentially related to D2. This medium-pressure
metamorphism reached its peak at P = ~5–6 kb, T = 650–750°C.

Hot oceanic island-arc mantle lithosphere acted as a heat source, which led
to the formation of syn-kinematic calc-alkaline mafic and ultramafic intrusions, i.e., the gabbros and peridotites of the Metagabbro Gneiss Suite (MGGS).

At ~468–467 Ma, the hot oceanic island arc upper plate, which was continuously moving northwards, provided the heat for widespread quartz
diorite-granite magmatism in southern Connemara (Figure 5.5). These syn-
kinematic granites intruded and enveloped the earlier formed gabbros and
the Dalradian metasedimentary and metavolcanic rocks. The high temperatures and lower pressures (due to rapid exhumation) led to regional thermal
metamorphism (Buchan style, M3) with significant partial melting of the
Dalradian metasediments (e.g., Cashel Schist Fm.) in southern Connemara.
The syn-D3 metamorphic event (M3 "Buchan-style") reached sillimanite
grade in the southern half of the complex. Granulite facies rocks are recorded
near the margins of the gabbros in the MGGS (see Chapter 4). The quartz
diorite-granite intrusions were converted to orthogneisses during this time
period. These events led to the assembly of the Metagabbro Gneiss Suite
(MGGS) in southern Connemara (Figure 5.5). An incipient Mannin thrust-
shear zone that eventually resulted in formation of the brittle Mannin thrust
may have formed during this time (Figure 5.5).

Subduction polarity reversal occurred between ~468 and 466 Ma coincident
with the syn-kinematic quartz diorite-granite magmatism and M3 metamorphism in southern Connemara. Between ~466 and 463 Ma the Mannin Thrust
(MT) formed moving the Metagabbro Gneiss Suite over the metarhyolites of
the Delaney Dome (DD) (Figure 5.6).

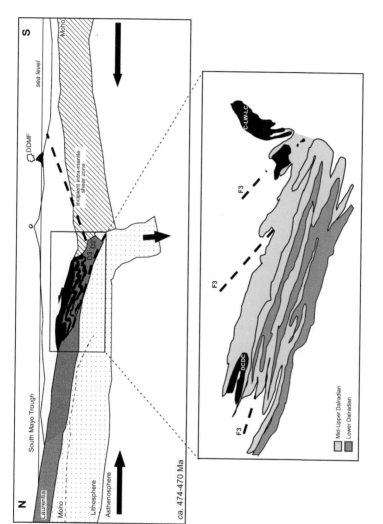

FIGURE 5.4

Schematic NW-SE profile of the collision zone at ~474–470 Ma with inset focusing on simplified structural patterns in the orogenic wedge. During this time, collision-related deformation events (D2 and D3) formed F2 and F3 folds. The syn-kinematic peridotite and gabbro intrusions (in black), i.e., the ~472 Ma Dawros-Currywongaun-Doughruagh Complex of northern Connemara (DCDC) and the ~470 Ma Cashel-Lough Wheelaun-Loughaunanny Complex (C-LW-LC) are depicted as being deformed by D3 in the inset above. The Dalradian was overridden northwards by (i) the Lough Nafooey Island arc and its South Mayo forearc basin (the South Mayo Trough); (ii) its frontal ophiolite complex (Deer Park Complex) and (iii) the accretionary complex (Killadangan Complex). The latter two are exposed further north in the Clew Bay area (Daly *et al.*, 2022; Ryan *et al.*, 2022).

(Adapted from Friedrich and Hodges, 2016. Abbreviation: DDMF: Delaney Dome Metarhyolite Formation.)

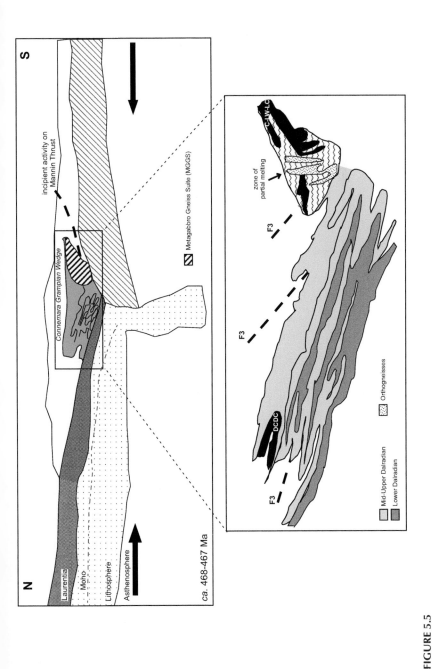

FIGURE 5.5

Schematic NW-SE cross-section of the collision zone at ~468–467 Ma and a focused view of the orogenic wedge (inset). Syn-kinematic quartz diorite-granite magmas (orthogneisses) intruded into the earlier formed gabbros in south Connemara forming the Metagabbro Gneiss Suite (MGGS). High-temperature (~750°C), lower-pressure (~3 kb) Buchan-style metamorphism (M3) led to migmatisation of the Dalradian strata. The initiation, at this time, of incipient activity on the Mannin Thrust is also posited by Friedrich and Hodges (2016).

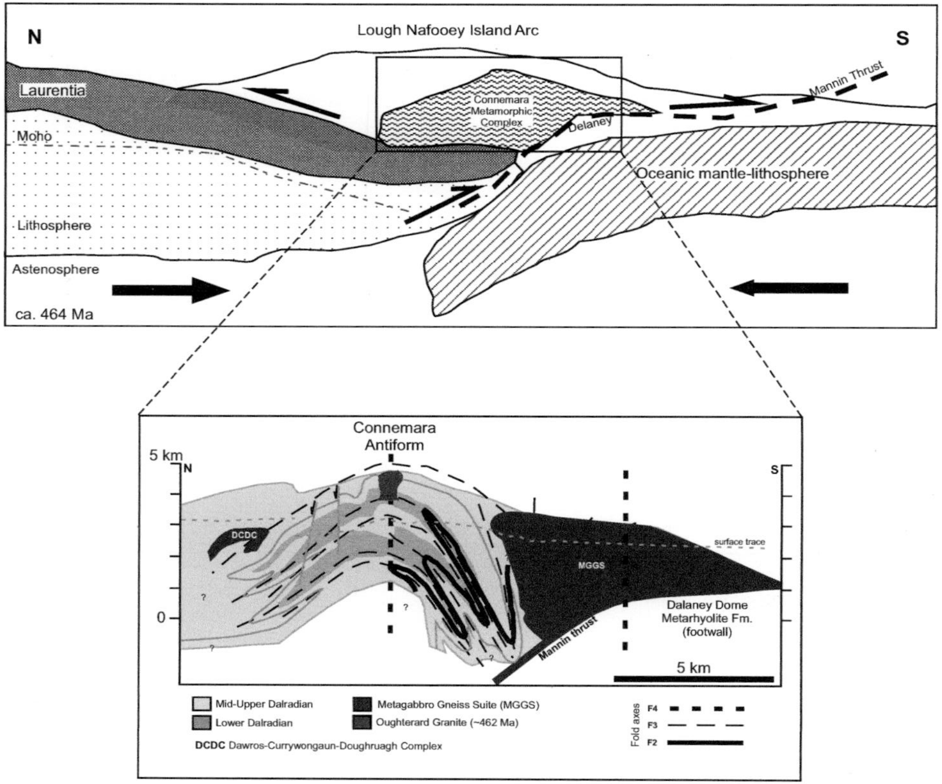

FIGURE 5.6
A schematic NW-SE cross-section and inset of the collision zone at ~464 Ma. Subduction polarity reversal occurs as the oceanic mantle-lithospheric plate now becomes the northerly directed down going plate. During this time the Mannin Thrust may have formed moving the Metagabbro Gneiss Suite over the rocks of the Delaney Dome Metarhyolite Formation. The location of the ~462 Ma Oughterard Granite is shown transecting the hinge region of the D4 Connemara antiform. Arrows indicate relative motion.

(Adapted from Friedrich and Hodges, 2016.)

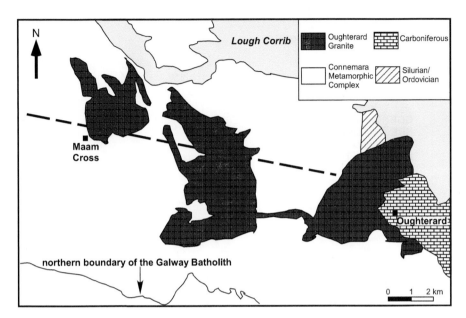

FIGURE 5.7
Geological map of the Oughterard Granite at the eastern end of the Connemara Metamorphic
Complex. The broken line indicates the axial trace of the D4 Connemara antiform which was
breached by the ~462 Ma Oughterard Granite. (Bradshaw *et al.*, 1969; Leake, 2023).

During this interval the regional-scale D4 Connemara antiform was
formed. Finally, the Oughterard Granite intruded into the hinge zone of
the D4 antiform at ~462 Ma (Bradshaw *et al.*, 1969; Friedrich and Hodges,
2016; Leake, 2023). The Oughterard Granite is located 3 km to 5 km to the
north of the Galway Batholith and occurs as three irregular bodies between
Maam Cross and Oughterard (Figure 5.7). Numerous smaller pods and
dikes extend to more than 15 km west of the main exposures. The granite is
pale grey and generally aphyric. Its mineralogy comprises quartz (30–50%),
albite-oligoclase (30–40%), microcline, chlorite after biotite and a little
muscovite (combined <7%). Leake (2023) presents new field, chemical and
Rb, Sr, S and Pb isotopic data that indicates the peraluminous Oughterard
Granite is of S-Type and formed by melting of the rocks belonging to the
Dalradian.

The CMC and Its Structural Setting in the Grampian
Terrane of NW Ireland and Scotland

The Connemara Metamorphic Complex is the only section of the Grampian
terrane that lies ~50 km to the south of the Highland Boundary Fault (Figure 5.8).
The Mannin Thrust was responsible for placing the whole of the high-grade

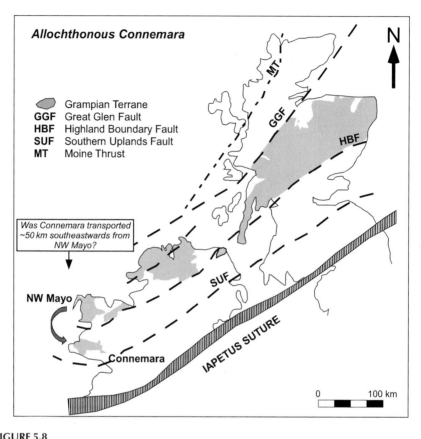

FIGURE 5.8
Regional map of NW Ireland and the UK showing the Grampian Terrane, major NE-SW fault lineaments and the Iapetus Suture. Connemara is the only part of the Grampian Terrane that lies south of the Highland Boundary Fault suggesting that Connemara is out of place, i.e., allochthonous and may have been transported south-eastwards from NW Mayo (~50 km) by the Mannin Thrust at ~454 Ma (upper Ordovician; Leake, 2021).

(Adapted from BGS 1:500.000 scale map Tectonic map of Britain, Ireland and adjacent areas (1996) and the BGS 1:625.000 scale Bedrock Geology map (UK North, 2007).)

rocks of the Connemara Metamorphic Complex above the lower-grade rocks of the Delaney Dome Metarhyolite Formation.

Geochronometry of the thrust-generated mylonitised Delaney Dome Metarhyolite Formation yields an age of 454 ± 4 Ma, i.e., Upper Ordovician (Leake, 2021). This age conflicts with the Friedrich and Hodges (2016) proposed model age of ~466–463 Ma for the Mannin Thrust (Figure 5.6) however, there is no published geochronometry to support this D4 age for the Mannin Thrust.

Geochronometry of the least deformed samples from the Delaney Dome Metarhyolite Formation yield a Lower Ordovician age of ~475 Ma, which is interpreted as the age of arc-volcanism, broadly similar to the arc-related gabbros of the Metagabbro Gneiss Suite (Draut and Clift, 2002; Leake, 2021). Furthermore, comparative geochemical studies indicate that the rocks of the Delaney Dome Metarhyolite Formation are similar to those of the nearby Tourmakeady Volcanic Group of the South Mayo Trough. They contain a 1 km thickness of rhyolites with the same Lower Ordovician age, and both have volcanic arc-like geochemistry (Draut and Clift, 2002; Leake, 2021). There is a spatial, temporal, and genetic link between all of these rhyolitic volcanic rocks and the magmatism that gave rise to the gabbros of the MGGS.

Pressure-Temperature-time (P-T-t) Paths

P-T-t paths illustrating the inferred metamorphic history of the CMC's metamorphic zones and their different heating paths, including tentative absolute ages for different phases of the metamorphism, were presented by Yardley *et al.* (1987) and Yardley (1989). The P-T-t paths show that initial medium-pressure Barrovian-style metamorphism was followed by high-T-low-P metamorphism, associated with synorogenic magmatism and ana-texis, generating different uplift and heating paths to produce the zonal sequences observed in the CMC.

P-T-t paths were presented by Friedrich and Hodges (2016) using PT data from Yardley *et al.* (1987) and Boyle and Dawes (1991) combined with geo-chronological results from Friedrich *et al.* (1999a, 1999b). Recently, Yardley and Cliff (2022) presented refined P-T-t paths that integrate their dataset of recalculated ages from existing geochronological ages in Tanner *et al.* (1989), Cliff *et al.* (1993), Cliff *et al.* (1996), Friedrich (1998), Friedrich *et al.* (1999a, 1999b), and Draut and Clift (2002). P-T-t paths, from Friedrich and Hodges (2016) and Yardley and Cliff (2022) are presented below (Figure 5.9).

The Friedrich and Hodges (2016) P-T-t Path

As referred to earlier, evidence for the D1 event is based on rare inclusion trails in garnet porphyroblasts. The clockwise trending blue dashed line (Figure 5.9) represents the Barrovian garnet zone in north Connemara. The red solid line represents the clockwise trending P-T-t path for the migmatite zone of south Connemara. This path tracks from ~472 Ma with the intrusion of the gabbros in NW Connemara and the regional D2 and M2 medium pressure, medium-temperature Barrovian-style metamorphism. These events were closely followed at ~470 Ma by the intrusion of the large gabbroic bodies

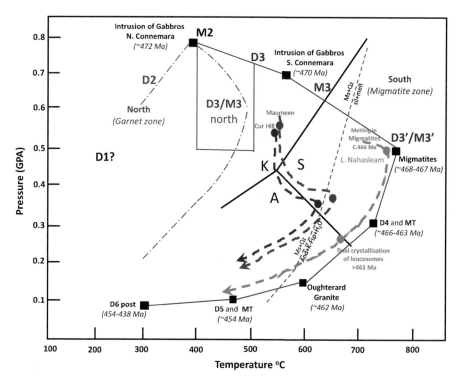

FIGURE 5.9

Pressure-Temperature-time (P-T-t) paths adapted from Yardley *et al.* (1987), Friedrich and Hodges (2016) and Yardley and Cliff (2022). The blue dashed line is the clockwise P-T path for the garnet zone of northern Connemara and the red line is based upon the P-T path for the migmatite zone in south Connemara after Friedrich and Hodges (2016). The latter tracks the deformation, magmatism and metamorphic events in Connemara starting with the intrusion of the gabbros in NW Connemara at ~472 Ma and following a clockwise path to D6 post 454–438 Ma. The Cur Hill (red), Maumeen (blue) and Lough Nahasleam (green) paths are from Yardley and Cliff (2022) (see Figure 2.1 for the locations), updated from Yardley *et al.* (1987) and Yardley and Warren (2021): filled circles on each of the three paths are the approximate P-T conditions of staurolite zone assemblages, peak metamorphism, and final crystallisation of the migmatite leucosomes. The Cur Hill (in the NE) to Maumeen (in the SW) path is from Excursion 1 and the Lough Nahasleam path is from Excursion 2 in Yardley and Cliff (2022). The recalculated ages of Yardley and Cliff (2022) are in green font and extend from ~466 Ma for melting in migmatites to ~461 Ma for final crystallisation of the leucosomes. The Al-silicate phase boundaries are from Richardson *et al.* (1969). Abbreviations: muscovite (Ms), andalusite (And), quartz (Qz), sillimanite (Sil), potassium feldspar (Kf).

in south Connemara and the D3 deformation event. Hydration during the emplacement of the gabbros converted them to amphibolites (metagabbros) containing hornblende and plagioclase. The M3 high-T-low-P metamorphism (Buchan-style metamorphism) is characterised by sillimanite-grade metamorphism in the Dalradian rocks. In south Connemara, syntectonic intrusions of quartz diorites and granites, into the Dalradian schists and the metagabbros caused partial melting to form migmatites that are assigned to M3'. D3' deformation of the quartz diorites, granites and migmatites created a suite of ortho- and paragneisses that are integral components of the Metagabbro Gneiss Suite. D4 followed, forming the regional-scale Connemara Antiform and the Mannin thrust. The Oughterard Granite was emplaced into the hinge zone of the D4 antiform at ~462 Ma. The Mannin thrust's position on the P-T-t path is the subject of much debate and occupies two points (encircled) on the P-T-t path in Figure 5.9. The 466–463 Ma position on the path is inferred from Friedrich and Hodges (2016) but without supporting geochronometry. However, geochronometry of the Mannin thrust mylonites provides a well-constrained late-Ordovician age (the D5 event ~454 ± 4 Ma. see Leake, 2021), indicating that the thrust is a late Grampian D5 event (Figure 5.9). Furthermore, Yardley and Cliff (2022) note that the final stage in the assembly of the Connemara massif came at 457 ± 3 Ma (a muscovite age from the Delaney Dome Metarhyolite Formation see Tanner *et al.*, 1989) when the arc intrusive sequence and its Dalradian basement were thrust over the Ordovician arc volcanics.

The Mannin thrust is folded by the E-W Mannin Antiform also part of the D5 event. Finally, the N-S Dolan Antiform (D6) is post 454 Ma and pre 438 Ma (Leake, 2021). It deformed the D5 Mannin Antiform and formed the domal architecture of the Delaney Dome. D6 also marks the development of regional fault movements throughout Connemara between the end-Ordovician and early Silurian times, i.e., post 454–438 Ma or later (Leake, 2021). These faults created basins into which the early Silurian sediments were deposited. According to Leake (2021), major D7 E-W striking Scandian folding, at ~426 Ma, of the Silurian rocks in north Connemara was accomplished by renewed strike faulting in the basement with vertical slip, facilitated by vertical foliation planes and renewed movement on NE-SW and NW-SE faults. These movements tightened the D4 Connemara Antiform, making it a D4-D7 composite structure (Badley, 2014). Finally, D7 movements uplifted the basement and its covering rocks, thus ending Silurian sedimentation. The D1 to D7 events are tabulated in Table 5.1. For completeness, event D8 is also included; however, this relates to the assembly of the Galway Granite Complex (GGC) which is detailed in Chapters 6–9.

The Yardley and Cliff (2022) Cur Hill-Maumeen P-T-t Path

The P-T-t paths for rocks from each end of the Cur Hill-Maumeen traverse in Excursion 1 (Yardley and Cliff, 2022), start from the inferred staurolite zone conditions (P ~ 550 MPa and *T* ~ 550°C). Andalusite, in the staurolite-sillimanite schists from Cur Hill, was partially replaced by sillimanite, reflecting a drop in pressure but then heating to move into the sillimanite field. The significance of this observation, according to Yardley and Cliff (2022),

TABLE 5.1

Tabulation of D1 to D8 Events Linked to Geochronology, Magmatism and Metamorphism. D8, the assembly of the Galway Granite Complex, is included for completeness

Deformation (d)	Fold (f)	Timing	Igneous Intrusions	Metamorphism
D1	No folds Microscopic Inclusion trails in Porphyroblasts	Pre-472 Ma		
D2	One major F2 fold (Derryclare fold) and minor F2 folds	~472–470 Ma	Gabbros converted to amphibolites	M2 Med P&T (Barrovian style)
D3	Most common open to isoclinal F3 folds	~470–467 Ma	Quartz diorites-granites converted to orthogneisses	M3 Low P-High T (Buchan style) Partial melting (migmatites)
D4	Major upright D4 antiforms (D4 Connemara Antiform)	~466–462 Ma		
		~462 Ma	Oughterard Granite	
D5	Mannin Thrust E-W Mannin Antiform	~454 Ma		
D6	N-S Dolan Antiform forming the Delaney Dome	Post 454–438 Ma		
D7	Scandian Tightening of Connemara Antiform (D4-D7 composite structure)	~426 Ma		
D8	Major Faults (Transpression and Transtension) NW-SE; E-W Faults	~425–380 Ma	Assembly of the Galway Granite Complex	Thermal Metamorphism of the GGC's country rocks. Hydrothermal Metamorphism of CMC, e.g., Serpentinisation of Marbles

Notes: Chapters 6 to 8 detail the events that occur during D8. Geochronology used here (D1 to D4) is from Friedrich and Hodges (2016) and Yardley and Cliff (2022), D5 to D7 from Leake (2021) and D8 from Feely *et al.* (2022).

is that it rules out a simple clockwise P-T-t path, indicating that uplift and erosion began to affect the rocks before heating from magma emplacement. Garnet-sillimanite schists from Maumeen at the SW end of the traverse did not develop andalusite and are inferred here (Figure 5.9) to have followed a similar path to the Cur Hill rocks but always lying within the sillimanite stability field.

The Yardley and Cliff (2022) Lough Nahasleam Migmatites P-T-t Path

The highest-grade migmatites, at Lough Nahasleam (Excursion 2; Yardley and Cliff, 2022), melted at a pressure near 500 MPa (Barber and Yardley, 1985) but were likely staurolite-kyanite schists initially (Leake and Tanner, 1994), so they must have experienced magmatic heating earlier in the history of uplift and erosion than the localities to the north. They remained hot and partially molten through the uplift event as some leucosomes crystallised in the andalusite field (Barber and Yardley, 1985). Overall, the metamorphic assemblages point to a drop in pressure indicative of the removal of 5–10 km of cover accompanying second phase folding and continuing deformation.

Finally, the geochronology used in Figure 5.9 shows broad agreement between the data published by Friedrich and Hodges (2016) and the recalculated ages of Yardley and Cliff (2022); however, it is recommended to read the detailed discussions on both the age determinations and the inferred interplay between deformation, metamorphism and magmatism in the CMC.

Finally, the evolution of the CMC is summarised by Yardley and Cliff (2022) as follows: the early metamorphic history of the CMC followed a medium-P (Barrovian) trend, like most other areas where Dalradian metasediments occur. This was followed in much of the region by high-T-low-P metamorphism driven by arc magmatism coupled to progressive uplift and erosion. The earlier medium-P assemblages are preserved in areas that were not heated further during the stage of arc magmatism. The last magmatic activity, which produced the Oughterard Granite at ~462 Ma, was emplaced shortly before Connemara was thrust over low-grade metarhyolites on the Mannin Thrust.

References

Badley, M.E. 2014. The Connemara Antiform and Its Possible Silurian History. *Irish Journal of Earth Sciences*, 32, 71–8.

Barber, J.P. and Yardley, B.W.D. 1985. Conditions of High-Grade Metamorphism in the Dalradian of Connemara, Ireland. *Journal of the Geological Society of London*, 142, 87–96.

Boyle, A.P. and Dawes, I.P. 1991. Contrasted Metamorphic and Structural Evolutions Across a Major Ductile/Brittle Displacement Zone in NW Connemara, Western Ireland. *Geologische Rundschau*, 80, 459–80.

Bradshaw, R., Plant, A.G., Burke, K.C. and Leake, B.E. 1969. The Oughterard Granite, Connemara, Co. Galway. *Proceedings of the Royal Irish Academy*, 68B, 39–65.

Chew, D.M. and Strachan, R.A. 2014. The Laurentian Caledonides of Scotland and Ireland. In: F. Corfu, D. Gasser and D.M. Chew (eds.) *New Perspectives on the Caledonides of Scandinavia and Related Areas*. Geological Society of London Special Publications, vol. 390. Geological Society, Burlington House, Piccadilly, London, UK, 45–91.

Cliff, R.A., Yardley, B.W.D. and Bussy, F. 1993. U-Pb Isotopic Dating of Fluid Infiltration and Metasomatism During Dalradian Regional Metamorphism in Connemara, Western Ireland. *Journal of Metamorphic Geology*, 11, 185–91.

Cliff, R.A., Yardley, B.W.D. and Bussy, F. 1996. U-Pb and Rb-Sr Geochronology of Magmatism and Metamorphism in the Dalradian of Connemara, Western Ireland. *Journal of the Geological Society of London*, 153, 109–20.

Daly, J.S., Chew, D.M., Flowerdew, M.J., Menuge, J.F., Fitzgerald, R., McAteer, C.A. and Scanlon, R. 2022. The Basement and Dalradian Rocks of the North Mayo Inlier. In: P.D. Ryan (ed.) *A Field Guide to the Geology of Western Ireland*. Springer Geology Field Guides. Springer Nature, Switzerland, 9–72. Print ISBN 978-3-030-97478-7.

Dewey, J.F. and Ryan, P.D.R. 2016. Connemara: Its Position and Role in the Grampian Orogeny. *Canadian Journal of Earth Sciences*, 53, 1246–57.

Draut, A.E. and Clift, P.D. 2002. The Origin and Significance of the Delaney Dome Formation, Connemara, Ireland. *Journal of the Geological Society, London*, 159, 95–103.

Feely, M., McCarthy, W., Costanzo, A., Leake, B.E.L. and Yardley, B.W.D. 2022. The Late Silurian to Upper Devonian Galway Granite Complex. In: P.D. Ryan (ed.) *A Field Guide to the Geology of Western Ireland*. Springer Geology Field Guides. Springer Nature, Switzerland, 303–62. Print ISBN 978-3-030-97478-7.

Friedrich, A.M. 1998. ^{40}Ar/^{39}Ar and U-Pb Geochronological Constraints on the Thermal and Tectonic Evolution of the Connemara Caledonides, Western Ireland. PhD thesis, Massachusetts Institute of Technology.

Friedrich, A.M., Bowring, S.A., Martin, M.W. and Hodges, K.V. 1999a. Short-Lived Continental Magmatic Arc at Connemara, Western Irish Caledonides: Implications for the Age of the Grampian Orogeny. *Geology*, 27, 27–30.

Friedrich, A.M. and Hodges, K.V. 2016. Geological Significance of ^{40}Ar/^{39}Ar Mica Dates Across a Mid-Crustal Continental Plate Margin, Connemara (Grampian Orogeny, Irish Caledonides), and Implications for the Evolution of Lithospheric Collisions. *Canadian Journal of Earth Sciences*, 53, 1258–78.

Friedrich, A.M., Hodges, K.V., Bowring, S.A. and Martin, M. 1999b. Geochronological Constraints on the Magmatic, Metamorphic and Thermal Evolution of the Connemara Caledonides, Western Ireland. *Journal of Geological Society of London*, 156, 1217–30.

Leake, B.E. 2021. The Geology of the Clifden District, Connemara Co. Galway, Ireland, and Present Understanding of Connemara Geology. *Irish Journal of Earth Sciences*, 39, 1–28.

Leake, B.E. 2023. New Light on the Oughterard Granite; Connemara's S-Type Granite, Ireland. *Irish Journal of Earth Sciences*, 41, 1–11.

Leake, B.E. and Tanner, P.W.G. 1994. *The Geology of the Dalradian and Associated Rocks of Connemara, Western Ireland*. Royal Irish Academy. 96p. ISBN 1-8740445-18-6.

Richardson, S.W., Gilbert, M.C. and Bell, P.M. 1969. Experimental Determination of Kyanite-Andalusite and Andalusite-Sillimanite Equilibrium; the Aluminium Silicate Triple Point. *American Journal of Science*, 267, 259–72.

Ryan, P.D., Dewey, J.F. and Graham, J.R. 2022. The Ordovician Fore-Arc and Arc Complex. In: P.D. Ryan (ed.) *A Field Guide to the Geology of Western Ireland*. Springer Geology Field Guides. Springer Nature, Switzerland, 179–228. Print ISBN 978-3-030-97478-7

Tanner, P.W.G., Dempster, T.J. and Dickin, A.P. 1989. Time of Docking of the Connemara Terrane with the Delaney Dome Formation, Western Ireland. *Journal of the Geological Society of London*, 146, 389.

Webster, D., Anderton, R. and Skelton, A. 2017. *A Guide to the Geology of Islay*. Ringwood Publishing. 188p. ISBN 978-1-901514-16-2.

Yardley, B.W.D. 1989. *An Introduction to Metamorphic Petrology*. Longman Earth Science Series. 249p. ISBN 0-582-30096-7.

Yardley, B.W.D., Barber, J. and Gray, J. 1987. The Metamorphism of the Dalradian Rocks of Western Ireland and Its Relation to Tectonic Setting. *Philosophical Transactions of the Royal Society of London A*, 321, 243–70.

Yardley, B.W.D. and Cliff, R.A. 2022. The Ordovician Arc Roots of Connemara. In: P.D. Ryan (ed.) *A Field Guide to the Geology of Western Ireland*. Springer Geology Field Guides. Springer Nature, Switzerland, 131–77. Print ISBN 978-3-030-97478-7.

Yardley B.W.D. and Warren, C.E. 2021. *An Introduction to Metamorphic Petrology*, 2nd edn. Cambridge University Press. 333.

6

The Galway Granite Complex (GGC): Geological Setting, Geochronology, Petrology, Geochemistry and Thermal Metamorphism

The Galway Granite Complex (GGC) comprises a suite of plutons called the Earlier Plutons: Roundstone, Inish, Omey and Letterfrack Plutons and the later Galway Batholith comprising the Carna and the Galway-Kilkieran Plutons. The granites of the GGC were emplaced into the Connemara Metamorphic Complex to the north, west and east, and into the Lower Ordovician South Connemara Group in the south. The Carboniferous limestones (~350 Ma) are in fault contact with the Galway-Kilkieran Pluton to the east. Gravity and magnetic data indicate that the GGC extends offshore, to the southwest, south and southeast, beneath the Carboniferous rocks of Galway Bay. U-Pb zircon and Re-Os molybdenite chronometry demonstrate that the formation of the GGC reflects five magmatic episodes that extended from ~423 Ma to at least ~380 Ma. The lithologies of the Galway Granite Complex define a continuum from diorites and quartz diorites to granodiorites and granites to the most evolved alkali feldspar granites. Major element trends indicate that the granites of the GGC display typical calc-alkaline variation trends.

The Geological Setting of the GGC

The Galway Granite Complex (GGC) comprises a suite of relatively minor plutons called the Earlier Plutons: Roundstone, Inish, Omey and Letterfrack Plutons and the later Galway Batholith that has two, larger plutons called the Carna and the Galway-Kilkieran Plutons (McCarthy *et al.*, 2015a, 2015b; Feely *et al.*, 2022). The latter pluton is here renamed the Galway-Kilkieran Pluton to reflect its ~50 km axial extent from Galway in the east to Kilkieran in the west. The granites of the GGC were emplaced into the Connemara Metamorphic Complex to the north, west and east, and into the Lower Ordovician South Connemara Group in the south (Max *et al.*, 1975; Leake and Tanner, 1994; Ryan and Dewey, 2004; Ryan and Dewey, 2022). The Carboniferous limestones (~350 Ma) are in fault contact with the Galway-Kilkieran Pluton to the east (Lees and Feely, 2016, 2017) (Figure 6.1). Gravity and magnetic data indicate that the GGC extends offshore, to the southwest, south and southeast, beneath the Carboniferous rocks of Galway Bay (Murphy, 1952; Fairhead and Walker, 1977; Max *et al.*, 1983).

DOI: 10.1201/9781032698410-6

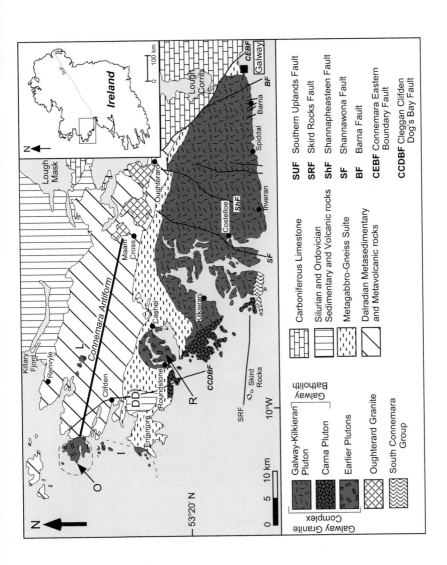

FIGURE 6.1
Geological map of the Galway Granite Complex and its environs. The spatial distribution of the Earlier Plutons (Omey (O), Inish (I), Roundstone (R) and Letterfrack (L) Plutons) and the Galway Batholith's Carna and Galway-Kilkieran Plutons is shown. The Metagabbro-Gneiss Suite and the Dalradian rocks are collectively termed, the Connemara Metamorphic Complex (CMC). The ~462 Ma Oughterard Granite intruded the rocks of

(*Continued*)

FIGURE 6.1   (CONTINUED)
the CMC. Silurian and Ordovician sedimentary and volcanic rocks are exposed to the north of the CMC. The Lower Ordovician South Connemara Group (metasedimentary and metavolcanic rocks) occur along a section of the exposed southern margin of the Galway Batholith. The Lower Ordovician Delaney Dome (DD) is composed of metarhyolites. To the east the Galway-Kilkieran Pluton is in faulted contact with Lower Carboniferous limestones (~350 Ma).

(Map adapted from Townend, 1966; Max *et al.*, 1978; Leake and Tanner 1994; Pracht *et al.*, 2004; Leake, 2006; Leake, 2011; Lees and Feely, 2016, 2017.)

The Geochronology of the GGC: Spatial and Temporal Relationships

U-Pb zircon and Re-Os molybdenite chronometry demonstrate that the formation of the GGC reflects five magmatic episodes that extended from ~423 Ma to at least ~380 Ma (Buchwaldt *et al.*, 2001; Feely *et al.*, 2003; Selby *et al.*, 2004; Feely *et al.*, 2007; Feely *et al.*, 2010, McCarthy, 2013, Feely *et al.*, 2018; Feely *et al.*, 2020) (Figure 6.2). The five episodes are: (1) emplacement

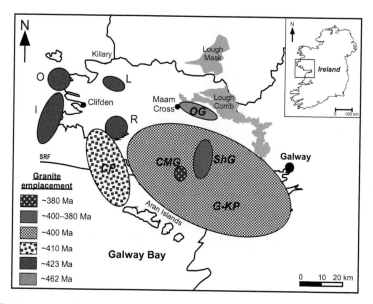

FIGURE 6.2
Schematic diagram showing the spatial and temporal distribution of the individual granite plutons of the Galway Granite Complex: Omey Pluton (O); Letterfrack Pluton (L); Inish Pluton (I); Roundstone Pluton (R); Carna Pluton (CP); Galway-Kilkieran Pluton (G-KP); Shannapheasteen granite (ShG) and Costelloe Murvey granite (CMG). The older ~462 Ma Oughterard Granite (OG) is also shown.

at ~423 Ma of the Earlier Plutons: Omey, Roundstone and Inish Plutons and the undated Letterfrack Pluton; (2) emplacement of the Carna Pluton at ~410 Ma followed by (3) emplacement of the Galway-Kilkieran Pluton at ~400 Ma; (4) later emplacement of the Costelloe Murvey Granite within the Galway-Kilkieran Pluton at ~380 Ma. The emplacement of the Shannaphaesteen Granite, whose age has not yet been determined, may be part of this event or indeed the ~400 Ma event, and (5) emplacement of a suite of late Devonian composite dolerite-rhyolite dikes (Mohr *et al.*, 2018). Furthermore, Johnson *et al.* (2011) also report a late Devonian U-Pb age (373.9 ± 4.0 Ma) for a GGC-related felsitic quartz porphyry dike located ~25 km to the north on Ben Levy.

Introduction to the Petrology and Mineralogy of the GGC

The granites of the GGC range from fine to coarse grained (<1 mm–5 cm) rocks, containing quartz, alkali and plagioclase feldspars with minor amounts (<5.0%) of mica (biotite and/or muscovite), hornblende, and accessory minerals (usually <1%) such as apatite, allanite, titanite (sphene) and zircon. Variations in mineral proportions are linked to a spectrum of granite hues ranging from pink to greyish white.

Orthoclase invariably forms large salmon pink phenocrysts (~5 cm) that are set in a relatively finer grained groundmass, i.e.: porphyritic texture. The orthoclase can display a mantle of white plagioclase feldspar called *rapakivi* texture which is common in mingled granite magmas a feature common in the Galway-Kilkieran Pluton (Baxter and Feely, 2002).

Granite Classification: A Mineralogical Perspective

Granites are classified according to the proportions of the essential rock-forming minerals: quartz, alkali feldspar (orthoclase and/or microcline and/or albite) and plagioclase feldspar that are present in the rock. Plotting the percentage of Q (Quartz), A (Alkali feldspar) and P (Plagioclase feldspar) onto the QAP ternary diagram (after Streckeisen, 1976) is the conventional method used to classify a range of plutonic igneous rock types including granites.

Granite (*sensu stricto*) contains both plagioclase and alkali feldspars. When alkali feldspar(s) (orthoclase ± microcline ± albite) dominate(s), the granite is classified as an *alkali feldspar granite*. When a granitic rock contains significantly more plagioclase than alkali feldspar it is defined as either a *granodiorite* or a *tonalite*. The term 'granite' (*sensu lato*), however, is commonly used to describe rock types that range from alkali feldspar granites to granites, granodiorites, quartz diorites and even diorites. The lithologies of the Galway Granite Complex define a continuum from diorites and quartz diorites to granodiorites and granites to the most evolved alkali feldspar granites. QAP ternary diagrams are used in Chapter 8 to illustrate the variations in the granite types that comprise the Earlier Plutons and the Carna and Galway-Kilkieran Plutons.

Geochemical Characteristics of the GGC

Major element trends using AFM ($Na_2O + K_2O$ wt.% - FeOt wt.% - MgO wt.%) and CNK (CaO wt.% - Na_2O wt.% - K_2O wt.%) ternary diagrams indicate that the granites of the GGC display typical calc-alkaline variation trends. The arrows in Figures 6.3a and b trace the differentiation from mafic diorites to the felsic granites. The bivariate plots of Rb ppm and Sr ppm (Figure 6.3c) and of Rb/Sr and TiO_2 wt.% (Figure 6.3d) display an increase in Rb ppm and Rb/Sr from the less evolved granites to the more fractionated granites.

The behaviour of the REE (Figure 6.3e) with granite evolution was established with reference to Si, Ti, Zr and Sr as fractionation indices by Feely *et al.* (1991). The granodiorites and granites show light REE rich patterns and the more evolved leucogranites, i.e., Murvey Granite are depleted in light REE and Eu and enriched in heavy REE. Light REE and especially Eu concentrations are significantly depleted in two of the leucogranites: Costelloe Murvey Granite and the garnetiferous Murvey Granite (see Chapter 9). They also show significant heavy REE enrichment developing distinctive gull winged REE profiles (Figure 6.3e). The behaviour of the REE in the granites of the GGC reflects the timing of accessory phase crystallisation. Light REE depletion is due to the early crystallisation (e.g., in less evolved granites and granodiorites) of light REE rich phases (e.g., allanite). Whereas the late crystallisation of xenotime, monazite, thorite and uraninite is in response to enrichment of heavy REE, Y, U and Th (Feely *et al.*, 1989) in the more evolved leucogranites. A tectonic discrimination diagram (Figure 6.3f) using relative abundances (ppm) of Hafnium (Hf), Tantalum (Ta) and Rubidium (Rb) places the granites of the GGC in the late and post-collisional tectonic field.

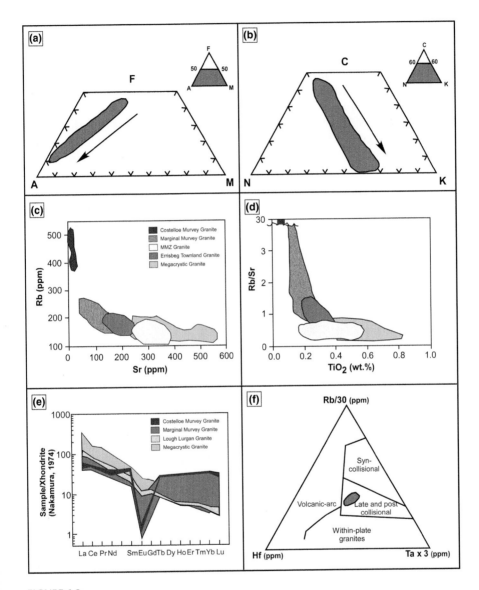

FIGURE 6.3
General geochemical characteristics and trends portrayed by the granites of the GGC. (a) AFM ($Na_2O + K_2O$ wt.% - FeOt wt.% - MgO wt.%). (b) CNK (CaO wt.% - Na_2O wt.% - K_2O wt.%). (c) Rb ppm and Sr ppm bivariate plot. (d) Rb/Sr and TiO_2 wt.% bivariate plot key as in (c). (e) Sample/ Chondrite (Nakamura, 1974) normalised REE profiles. (f) A tectonic discrimination diagram indicating that the granites of the GGC plot in the field defined by late-and post-collisional granites.

(Data adopted from Feely and Madden, 1988; Feely *et al.*, 1989; Feely *et al.*, 1991; El Desouky *et al.*, 1996; Feely *et al.*, 2006.)

Thermal Metamorphism: Aureole Rocks of the GGC

The Earlier Plutons (Omey, Roundstone, Inish and Letterfrack Plutons) were emplaced into the rocks of the Connemara Metamorphic Complex (CMC). Contact metamorphism overprints the two metamorphic events (M2 and M3 – see Chapter 4) recorded by the Dalradian rocks of the CMC during the Grampian Orogeny. The Letterfrack Pluton intruded the Streamstown Schist and Lakes Marble Formations (Leake and Tanner, 1994). Close to the granite contacts, andalusite porphyroblasts are developed in the pelitic rocks. The aureole rocks of the Inish Pluton contain cordierite and andalusite porphyroblasts in Dalradian pelitic hornfels (Townend, 1966; Cobbing, 1969). The Roundstone Pluton intruded rocks belonging to the MGGS and does not display significant contact metamorphism (Leake and Tanner, 1994). The contact metamorphism associated with the Omey Pluton's aureole rocks is well documented by Ferguson and Harvey (1979) and Ferguson and Al-Ameen (1985). These authors document thermally overprinted pelites and carbonates of the Streamstown Schist and Lakes Marble Formations displaying andalusite hornfels and spectacular wollastonite + grossular + vesuvianite + diopside bearing skarns see Feely *et al.* (2022).

According to Leake and Tanner (1994), there is insignificant contact metamorphism along the northern contact of the Galway Batholith because it intruded the rocks of the Metagabbro Gneiss Suite (MGGS; Figure 6.1). Granite temperatures were insufficient to trigger metamorphic reactions in the amphibolites of the MGGS. However, andalusite hornfels occur in the pelitic migmatites within the thermal aureole along the northern contact (Senior, 1973; Leake and Tanner, 1994). Andalusite and cordierite hornfels are locally developed in Dalradian pelitic horizons.

Along the southern contact, andalusite and cordierite hornfels occur in the pelitic rocks of the Lower Ordovician South Connemara Group. Ryan and Dewey (2022) describe pelitic lithologies, exposed on the western foreshore of Lettermullan Island, displaying spotting due to millimetric-scale sericitised cordierite porphyroblasts (Figure 6.4). Interbedded volcanic horizons are amphibolites and contain hornblende, plagioclase, diopside and calcic garnet (Ryan and Dewey, 2022). The emplacement of the Oughterard Granite at ~462 Ma., in the east, may have led to further growth of andalusite (Leake and Tanner, 1994); however, Yardley and Cliff (2022) state that the andalusite here could arguably be considered as thermal rather than regional.

Chapters 7–9 demonstrate how the exposures of the Galway Granite Complex afford endless opportunities to study granite mineralogy, and the geological processes responsible for the generation, ascent and emplacement of granites into the upper reaches of the crust during the collision of Laurentia with Avalonia.

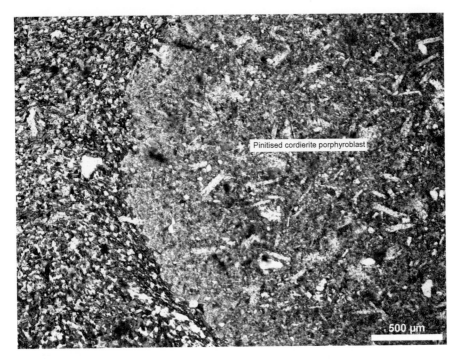

Pinitised cordierite porphyroblast

500 μm

FIGURE 6.4
Photomicrograph (PPL) of a pinitised cordierite porphyroblast in a hornfels from the South
Connemara Group, Lettermullan Island. The cordierite contains discernable randomly orien-
tated sericite flakes (53.231890°, −9.746154°).

References

Baxter, S. and Feely, M. 2002. Magma Mixing and Mingling Textures in Granitoids:
Examples from the Galway Granite, Connemara, Ireland. *Mineralogy and Petrology*,
76, 63–67.

Buchwaldt, R., Kroner, A., Toulkeredes, T., Todt, W. and Feely, M. 2001. Geochronology
and Nd-Sr Systematics of Late Caledonian Granites in Western Ireland: New
Implications for the Caledonian Orogeny. *Geological Society of America*, 33(1), A32.

Cobbing, E.J. 1969. The Geology of the District North-West of Clifden, Co Galway
Proceedings of the Royal Irish Academy, 67B, 303–25.

El Desouky, M., Feely, M. and Mohr P. 1996. Diorite-Granite Magma Mingling and
Mixing Along the Axis of the Galway Granite Batholith, Ireland. *Journal of the
Geological Society of London*, 153, 361–74.

Fairhead, J.D. and Walker, P. 1977. The Geological Interpretation of Gravity and
Magnetic Surveys Over the Exposed Southern Margin of the Galway Granite,
Ireland. *Geological Journal*, 12, 17–24.

Feely, M., Coleman, D., Baxter, S. and Miller, B. 2003. U-Pb Zircon Geochronology of the Galway Granite, Connemara, Ireland: Implications for the Timing of Late Caledonian Tectonic and Magmatic Events and for Correlations with Acadian Plutonism in New England. *Atlantic Geology*, 39, 175–84.

Feely, M., Costanzo, A., Gaynor, S.P., Selby, D. and McNulty, E. 2020. A Review of Molybdenite, and Fluorite Mineralisation in Caledonian Granite Basement, Western Ireland, Incorporating New Field and Fluid Inclusion Studies, and Re-Os and U-Pb Geochronology. *Lithos*, 354–355, 1–12.

Feely, M., Gaynor, S., Venugopal, N., Hunt, J. and Coleman, D.S. 2018. New U-Pb Zircon Ages for the Inish Granite Pluton, Galway Granite Complex, Connemara, Western Ireland. *Irish Journal of Earth Sciences*, 36(1), 1–7.

Feely, M., Leake, B. E., Baxter, S., Hunt, J., Mohr, P. 2006. *A Geological Guide to the Granites of the Galway Batholith, Connemara, Western Ireland*. Geological Survey of Ireland, Field guides Series, Geological Survey of Ireland, Dublin, 70p. ISBN 1-899702-56-3.

Feely, M. and Madden, J. 1988. Trace Element Variation in the Leucogranites Within the Main Galway Granite, Connemara, Ireland. *Mineralogical Magazine*, 52, 139–46.

Feely, M., McCabe, E. and Kunzendorf, H. 1991. The Evolution of REE Profiles in the Galway Granite, Western Ireland. *Irish Journal of Earth Sciences*, 11, 71–89.

Feely, M., McCabe, E. and Williams, C.T. 1989. U, Th and REE Bearing Accessory Minerals in a High Heat Production (HHP) Leucogranite Within the Galway Granite, Western Ireland. *Transactions. Institution of Mining and Metallurgy*, 98, B27–B32.

Feely, M., McCarthy, W., Costanzo, A., Leake, B. E. and Yardley, B.W.D. 2022. The Late Silurian to Upper Devonian Galway Granite Complex. In: P.D. Ryan (ed.) *A Field Guide to the Geology of Western Ireland*. Springer Geology Field Guides. Springer Nature, Switzerland, 303–362. Print ISBN 978-3-030-97478-7.

Feely, M., Selby, D., Conliffe, J. and Judge, M. 2007. Re-Os Geochronology and Fluid Inclusion Microthermometry of Molybdenite Mineralisation in the Late-Caledonian Omey Granite, Western Ireland. *Applied Earth Science: Transactions of the Institution of Mining and Metallurgy: Section B*, 116(3), 143–149.

Feely, M., Selby, D., Hunt, J. and Conliffe, J. 2010. Long-Lived Granite-Related Molybdenite Mineralization at Connemara, Western Irish Caledonides. *Geological Magazine*, 147(6), 886–894.

Ferguson, C.C. and Al-Ameen, S.I. 1985. Muscovite Breakdown and Corundum Growth at Anomalously Low fH₂O: A Study of Contact Metamorphism and Convective Fluid Movement Around the Omey Granite, Connemara, Western Ireland. *Mineralogical Magazine*, 49, 505–515.

Ferguson, C.C. and Harvey, P.K. 1979. Thermally Overprinted Dalradian Rocks Near Cleggan, Connemara, Western Ireland. *Proceedings of the Geologists' Association London*, 90, 43–50.

Johnson, E.A., Sutherland, C., Logan, M.A.V., Samson, S.D. and Feely, M. 2011. Emplacement Conditions of a Porphyritic Felsite Dyke and Timing of Motion Along the Coolin Fault at Ben Levy, Co. Galway. *Irish Journal of Earth Sciences*, 29, 1–13.

Leake, B.E. 2006. Mechanism of Emplacement and Crystallisation History of the Northern Margin and Centre of the Galway Granite, Western Ireland. *Transactions of the Royal Society of Edinburgh: Earth Sciences*, 97, 1–23.

Leake, B.E. 2011. Stoping and the Mechanisms of Emplacement of the Granites in the Western Ring Complex of the Galway Granite Batholith, Western Ireland. *Earth and Environmental Science Transactions of the Royal Society of Edinburgh*, 102, 1–16.

Leake, B.E. and Tanner, P.W.G. 1994. *The Geology of the Dalradian and Associated Rocks of Connemara, Western Ireland*. Royal Irish Academy. 96p. ISBN 1-874045-18-6.

Lees, A. and Feely, M. 2016. The Connemara Eastern Boundary Fault: A Review and Assessment Using New Evidence. *Irish Journal of Earth Sciences*, 34, 1–25.

Lees, A. and Feely, M. 2017. The Connemara Eastern Boundary Fault: A Correction. *Irish Journal of Earth Sciences*, 35, 55–6.

Max, M.D., Long, C.B. and Geoghegan, M. 1978. The Galway Granite and Its Setting. *Geological Survey of Ireland Bulletin*, 2, 223–33.

Max, M.D., Long, C.B., Keary, R., Ryan, P.D., Geoghegan, M., O'Grady, M., Inamdar, D.D., McIntyre, T. and Williams, C.E. 1975. *Preliminary Report on the Geology of the Northwestern Approaches to Galway Bay and Part of Its Landward Area*. Geol. Survey Ireland, Report Series RS75/3, Geological Survey of Ireland, Dublin.

Max, M.D., Ryan, P.D. and Inamdar, D.D. 1983. A Magnetic Deep Structural Geology Interpretation of Ireland. *Tectonics*, 2, 431–51.

McCarthy, W. 2013. An Evaluation of Orogenic Kinematic Evolution Utilizing Crystalline and Magnetic Anisotropy in Granitoids. PhD thesis, University College Cork, National University of Ireland.

McCarthy, W., Petronis, M.S., Reavy, R.J. and Stevenson, C.T. 2015a. Distinguishing Diapirs from Inflated Plutons: An Integrated Rock Magnetic Fabric and Structural Study on the Roundstone Pluton, Western Ireland. *Journal of the Geological Society of London*, 172, 550–65.

McCarthy, W., Reavy, R.J., Stevenson, C.T. and Petronis, S. 2015b. Late Caledonian Transpression and the Structural Controls on Pluton Construction; New Insights from the Omey Pluton, Western Ireland. *Earth and Environmental Science Transactions of the Royal Society of Edinburgh*, 106(1), 11–28.

Mohr, P., Hunt, J., Riekstins, H. and Kennan, P.S. 2018. Distinguishing Dolerite Dike Populations in Post-Grampian Connemara. *Irish Journal of Earth Sciences*, 36, 1–16.

Murphy, T. 1952. Measurements of Gravity in Ireland: Gravity Survey of Central Ireland. *Dublin Institute for Advanced Studies, Geophysics Memoirs*, 2(Part 3), 31p.

Nakamura, N. 1974. Determination of REE, Ba, Fe, Mg, Na and K in Carbonaceous and Ordinary Chondrites. *Geochimica et Cosmochimica Acta*, 38, 757–75.

Pracht, M., Lees, A., Leake, B., Feely, M., Long, B., Morris J. and McConnell, B. 2004. Geology of Galway Bay: A geological description to accompany the Bedrock Geology 1:100,000 Scale Map Series, Sheet 14, Galway Bay. *Geological Survey of Ireland*. 76p., Geological Survey of Ireland, Dublin.

Ryan, P.D. and Dewey, J.F. 2004. The South Connemara Group Reinterpreted: A Subduction-Accretion Complex in the Caledonides of Galway Bay, Western Ireland. *Journal of Geodynamics*, 37, 513–29.

Ryan P.D. and Dewey, J.F. 2022. The South Connemara Group. In: P.D. Ryan (ed.) *A Field Guide to the Geology of Western Ireland*. Springer Geology Field Guides. 229–44. Springer Nature, Switzerland, Print ISBN 978-3-030-97478-7

Selby, D., Creaser, R.A. and Feely, M. 2004. Accurate Re-Os Molybdenite Dates from the Galway Granite, Ireland. A Critical Comment to: Disturbance of the Re-Os Chronometer of Molybdenites from the Late-Caledonian Galway Granite, Ireland, by Hydrothermal Fluid Circulation. *Geochemical Journal*, 38, 291–94.

Senior, A. 1973. The Geology of the Shannavara District, Connemara, Eire. PhD thesis University of Bristol.

Streckeisen, A. 1976. To Each Plutonic Rock Its Proper Name. *Earth-Science Reviews*, 12, 1–33.

Townend, R. 1966. The Geology of Some Granite Plutons from Western Connemara, Co. Galway. *Proceedings of the Royal Irish Academy*, 65B, 157–202.

Yardley, B.W.D. and Cliff, R.A. 2022. The Ordovician Arc Roots of Connemara. In: P.D. Ryan (ed.) *A Field Guide to the Geology of Western Ireland*. Springer Geology Field Guides. 131–77. Springer Nature, Switzerland, Print ISBN 978-3-030-97478-7.

7

Structural Controls on the Assembly of the Galway Granite Complex

The generation of the Late Silurian to Upper-Devonian granite magmas in Connemara can be accounted for by subduction-related slab dehydration, slab break-off and crustal thickening during the convergence of Avalonia, Baltica and Laurentia and later decompression due to Devonian transtension. During the slab breakoff of the eastern Avalonian plate, in the collision zone between Avalonia and Laurentia, the asthenosphere moved upwards, triggering extended and episodic deep crustal melting to produce the magmas that formed the Galway Granite Complex. Episodic magmatism extended over ~43 Ma (from ~423 Ma to ~380 Ma). Major SW-NE sinistral strike-slip crustal faults (e.g., the Great Glen, Highland Boundary and the Southern Uplands Faults) that parallel the Iapetus suture were active during the closure of the Iapetus Ocean. There are many examples of Irish and UK late-Caledonian (c. 430 to 380 Ma) granites, including those of the GGC, whose emplacement was controlled by transtension or transpression acting across this sinistral SW-NE strike-slip regime. A tectonic kinematic model is presented that invokes anticlockwise block rotation during transpression which triggered dilation zones. These were exploited by the Earlier Plutons. The Galway Batholith's Carna Pluton (~410 Ma) was intruded during a sinistral transpressive tectonic regime; a change to a transtension regime marks the emplacement of the later Galway-Kilkieran Pluton (~400 Ma). The Costelloe Murvey Granite (CMG) was emplaced into the Galway-Kilkieran Pluton at 380.1 ± 5 Ma and postdates all other granites in this pluton by ~20–15 Ma. This intrusion may not be related to the Caledonian Orogeny but likely related to some later magmatic event, e.g., the closure of the Rheic Ocean.

Iapetus Ocean Closure and Granite Magma Generation

From Late Silurian to Upper Devonian, an extensive suite of granite plutons was emplaced into the Laurentian crust of Ireland and the UK. This major phase of granite magmatism, including the Galway Granite Complex, was broadly coincident with the collisions between Laurentia, Baltica and

DOI: 10.1201/9781032698410-7

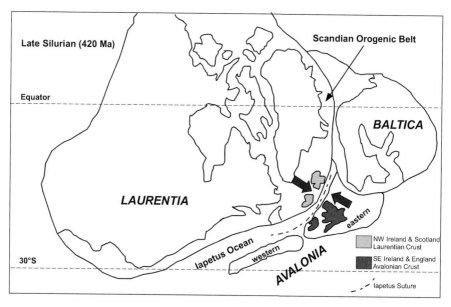

FIGURE 7.1

A Late Silurian plate tectonic configuration, post the collision between Baltica and Laurentia (in the NE) that triggered the Scandian Orogeny. Avalonian SE Ireland and England collide with Laurentian NW Ireland and Scotland forming the Iapetus suture. Acadian Orogeny was triggered by western Avalonia colliding with Laurentia and is represented today, for example, by the rocks of Newfoundland, Nova Scotia and New England. Red arrows indicate relative plate movement.

(Adapted from Chew and Strachan, 2014.)

Avalonia that led to the closure of the Iapetus Ocean and the formation of the Iapetus suture. During the late Silurian (~430–418 Ma) the collision between Baltica and Laurentia closed the northern part of the Iapetus Ocean initiating the Scandian Orogeny. The final closure of the Iapetus Ocean occurred when Laurentia collided with Avalonia (Figure 7.1).

Generation of the GGC's Magmas

The generation of the Late Silurian to Upper-Devonian granite magmas in Connemara can be accounted for by subduction-related slab dehydration, slab break-off and crustal thickening during the convergence of Avalonia, Baltica and Laurentia (Atherton and Ghani, 2002; Neilson *et al.*, 2009; Archibald and Murphy, 2021; Archibald *et al.*, 2021) and later decompression due to Devonian transtension (Brown *et al.*, 2008). During the slab break-off of the eastern Avalonian plate, in the collision zone between Avalonia and Laurentia, the asthenosphere moved upwards. This triggered extended and episodic deep crustal melting producing the magmas that formed the Galway Granite Complex. Episodic magmatism extended over ~43 Ma (from ~423 Ma to ~380 Ma; Figure 7.2).

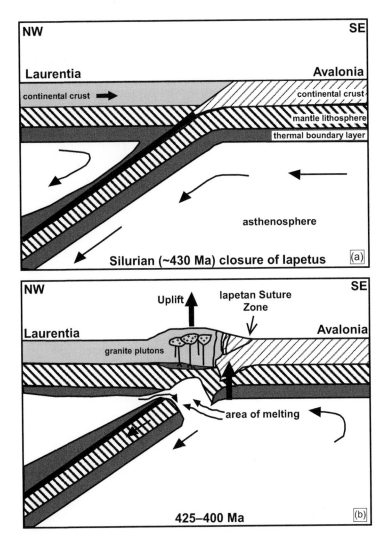

FIGURE 7.2

Schematics, adapted from Atherton and Ghani (2002), show slab breakoff on collision of Avalonia with Laurentia and the generation of granite magmas from Late-Silurian to Upper Devonian times including Connemara's GGC. (a) Subduction of eastern Avalonia under Laurentia during final closure of the Iapetus Ocean. (b) Eastern Avalonian slab breaks away and sinks. Melting, caused by the rise of the asthenosphere under the lithosphere in the collision zone, generates granite magmas that ascend to their emplacement zones in the upper part of the Laurentian crust. Arrows indicate plate movement directions.

Structural Controls on the Ascent of the GGC's Magmas

Major SW-NE sinistral strike-slip crustal faults (e.g., the Great Glen, Highland Boundary and the Southern Uplands Faults) that parallel the Iapetus suture were active during the closure of the Iapetus Ocean (Figure 7.3). There are many examples of Irish and UK late-Caledonian (c. 430 to 380 Ma) granites, including those of the GGC, whose emplacement was controlled by transtension or transpression (Dewey *et al.*, 1998) acting across this sinistral SW-NE strike-slip regime.

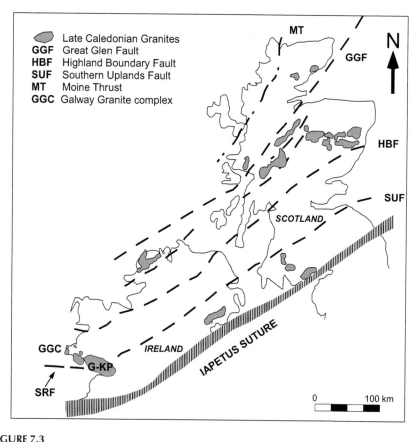

FIGURE 7.3

Map of NW Ireland and Scotland showing the outcrops of the Late Caledonian granites (430–380 Ma) northwest of the Iapetus suture and their spatial relationships to the major orogen parallel faults. The Galway-Kilkieran Pluton (G-KP) is spatially and genetically related to the sinistral strike-slip Southern Uplands Fault (SUF) that extends into Galway Bay where it is called the Skird Rocks Fault (Leake, 1978).

(Adapted from Atherton and Ghani, 2002; Dewey and Strachan, 2003.)

Changes in the regional late-Caledonian transcurrent stress field from transpression to transtension regimes are thought to have controlled the construction of the GGC (McCarthy, 2013). McCarthy *et al.* (2015a, 2015b) identified two sets of fabrics in the GGC: (1) NNW-SSE subvertical magmatic fabric, consistent with regional transpression, is recorded in the ~423 Ma Earlier Plutons (e.g., Omey and Roundstone Plutons) and (2) a WNW-ESE sub-horizontal magmatic fabric in the later Galway Batholith is consistent with regional transtension. A tectonic kinematic model for the construction of the GGC (Figure 7.4a and b) depicts the Connemara region as a deformation zone bounded by the Highland Boundary Fault (HBF) in the north and by the Skird Rocks Fault (SRF) in the south. The latter is a splay of the Southern Uplands Fault (Leake, 1978). Faults, oblique to the orogen, are the Cleggan-Clifden-Dog's Bay Fault (Leake and Tanner, 1994) and the Connemara Eastern Boundary Fault (Lees and Feely, 2016, 2017) – Figure 7.4.

Anticlockwise block rotation, during late Caledonian transpression, triggered dilation along NNW-SSE Faults. These dilation zones were exploited by the ascending Earlier Plutons, i.e., the Omey, and Roundstone Plutons. They yield U-Pb zircon and Re-Os molybdenite ages between ~425 and 420 Ma (Feely *et al.*, 2022) and possess steeply inclined NW-SE striking magnetic foliations (McCarthy *et al.*, 2015a, 2015b). The ~420 Ma Inish Pluton (Feely *et al.*, 2018) and the undated Letterfrack Pluton are also members of this suite.

The Galway Batholith's Carna Pluton occurs along the NNW-SSE Cleggan-Clifden-Dog's Bay Fault and has a prominent NNW-SSE subvertical fabric. The younger Carna Pluton (~410 Ma; Feely *et al.*, 2010) was intruded during this sinistral transpressive tectonic regime. The Carna Pluton was emplaced along the intersection of the Cleggan-Clifden-Dog's Bay Fault and the Skird Rocks Fault. A change to a regional transtension regime is marked by the emplacement of the ~400 Ma Galway Batholith's Galway-Kilkieran Pluton. Field, petrographic and magnetic data reveal magmatic state sub-horizontal foliations and sub-horizontal ESE-WNW lineations across the centre of the Galway-Kilkieran Pluton (Baxter *et al.*, 2005; McCarthy, 2013). McCarthy (2013) interpreted these fabrics as representing the switching of the stress directions sigma 1 (σ_1) and sigma 2 (σ_2), bringing σ_1 from the horizontal, i.e., regional transpression, to the vertical plane (*regional transtension*). The larger size of the Galway-Kilkieran Pluton coupled with granite heterogeneity, e.g., the magma mingling zone (El-Desouky *et al.*, 1996; Crowley and Feely, 1997; Baxter and Feely, 2002; Feely *et al.*, 2010) are interpreted to reflect increased volumes of magma emplacement as it migrated along the Skird Rocks Fault (Leake, 1978), a deep-seated, orogen parallel structure which was within the transtensional regime at ~400 Ma.

The Costelloe Murvey Granite (CMG) was emplaced into the Galway-Kilkieran Pluton at 380.1 ± 5.5 (Feely *et al.*, 2003), and postdates all other granites in this pluton by ~20–15 Ma. Buchwaldt *et al.* (2001) presented a Sr-Nd isotopic model that suggests that the CMG was generated by melting

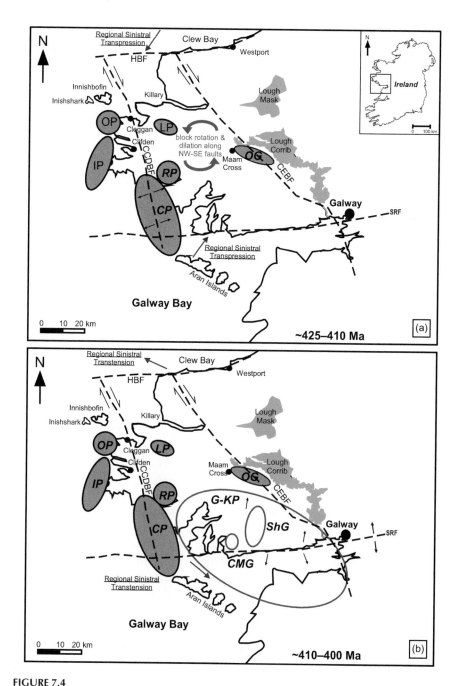

FIGURE 7.4
A schematic tectonic kinematic model for the construction of the GGC modified from McCarthy (2013) and Feely *et al.* (2022). In this construction the Barna Fault is replaced by the Connemara Eastern Boundary Fault. (a) Tectonic kinematic model from ~425 to 410 Ma. Anticlockwise

FIGURE 7.4 (CONTINUED)
vertical axis block rotation during late Caledonian transpression caused dilation zones to form facilitating the ascent of the Earlier Plutons. The Carna Pluton is spatially related to the Cleggan-Clifden-Dog's Bay Fault (CCDBF) and was emplaced during the transpressive regime. (b) A change to a regional transtension regime is linked to the emplacement of the Galway Batholith's ~400 Ma Galway-Kilkieran Pluton. Upper Devonian emplacement of the CMG occurred at ~380 Ma. The undated Shannapheasteen Granite (ShG) may be temporally related to the Costelloe Murvey Granite (CMG). Abbreviations: HBF: Highland Boundary Fault; CEBF: Connemara Eastern Boundary Fault; SRF: Skird Rocks Fault; OP: Omey Pluton; IP: Inish Pluton; RP: Roundstone Pluton; LP: Letterfrack Pluton; CP: Carna Pluton; G-KP: Galway-Kilkieran Pluton.

of older granite in the Galway-Kilkieran Pluton and notes that its geochemical fingerprint is quite distinct when compared to other members of the GGC. This intrusion may not be related to the Caledonian Orogeny but likely related to some later magmatic event, e.g., the closure of the Rheic Ocean (Domeier, 2016). The undated Shannapheasteen Granite (Leake, 2006) may be related in time to the emplacement of the CMG. Leake (2006) notes that the Shannapheasteen Granite, a fine-grained granodiorite, transects the magmatic fabrics in the suite of ~400 Ma granites of the Galway-Kilkieran Pluton.

A comparison of emplacement ages with calculated volumes (expressed as outcrop areas of individual plutons per km^2) of UK and Irish Caledonian granites (Figure 7.5) indicates that relatively large volumes of granite were intruded between the Scandian and Acadian Orogenies. The magmatism that formed the plutons of the Galway Granite Complex extended from late Scandian to post-Acadian times or from Silurian to Upper Devonian times (Figure 7.5). Regional transpression during the Scandian Orogeny equates with the emplacement of the Earlier Plutons. However, the Carna Pluton is also linked to a regional transpressive regime, and the Galway-Kilkieran Pluton was emplaced during a regional transtension regime (Figure 7.4b).

Figure 7.5 also indicates a transpressive regime during the emplacement of the Earlier Plutons. However, the Carna Pluton emplacement equates with a regional transtension regime (not transpressive as in Figure 7.4) and the emplacement of the Galway-Kilkieran Pluton equates with a regional transpression regime (not transtension as in Figure 7.4). These apparent temporal and tectonic regime contradictions serve to underline the conclusions of Woodcock *et al.* (2019) that long-range tectonic terrane correlations are imperfect along the Appalachian–Caledonian orogen and that Acadian events in the two sectors may correlate poorly both in time and by formation mechanism. Woodcock *et al.* (2007) attributed the Acadian deformation in the Caledonides to collision of Iberia/Armorica with Avalonia at about 400–390 Ma. The Acadian event in the Appalachians is now ascribed to accretion of Avalonia to Ganderia at about 420–400 Ma, followed by a Neoacadian event due to accretion of Meguma with Ganderia at 395–350 Ma (van Staal *et al.*, 2009; Wilson *et al.*, 2017). The emplacement of the Earlier Plutons (~420 Ma) and the

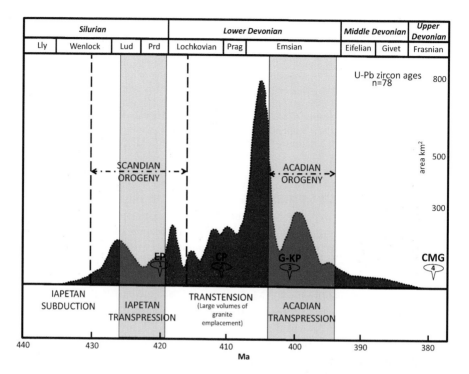

FIGURE 7.5

Plot of granite emplacement age data for UK and Irish Caledonian granites weighted against the outcrop area of individual plutons. The plutons of the Galway Granite Complex are shown as follows: Earlier Plutons: (1) EP; Carna Pluton: (2) CP; Galway-Kilkieran Pluton: (3) G-KP and the Upper Devonian, Costelloe Murvey Granite: (4) CMG.

(Diagram adapted from Miles *et al.*, 2016; Woodcock *et al.*, 2019.)

emplacement of GGC's Carna Pluton (~410 Ma) and Galway-Kilkieran Pluton (~400 Ma) equate in time with the Acadian event in the Appalachians and the emplacement of the ~380 Ma Costelloe Murvey Granite equates with the Neoacadian. Table 5.1 in Chapter 5, however, indicates that the assembly of the GGC equates to the D8 (~425 to 380 Ma) in Connemara (after Leake, 2021; Feely *et al.*, 2022) after Scandian fold tightening at~426 Ma.

Ballooning and Block Stoping in the GGC

Detailed field and microstructural studies of mineral fabrics in the Galway Batholith provide insights into the relationship between emplacement-related deformation and crystallisation state (Baxter *et al.*, 2005). Indeed, through-out the plutons that comprise the Galway Granite Complex, emplacement-related fabrics linked to lateral expansion (i.e., ballooning) operating in successive magma batches at the emplacement level are documented by several authors (e.g., El-Desouky *et al.*, 1996; McCarthy *et al.*, 2015a, 2015b; Leake, 2006). Field evidence for ballooning (Figure 7.6) and block stoping (Figure 7.7) is displayed by the granites of the GGC.

Detailed mapping of the plutons' contacts with the country rocks demon-strates that granite emplacement at roof level commonly occurred by block stoping of the country rocks. The contact zones around the GGC display many examples of arrested stoped blocks of country rock. Kilometric scale stoped blocks of rocks belonging to the Metagabbro Gneiss Suite injected and engulfed by the ascending granite magma are commonplace along sections of the Galway-Kilkieran Pluton's northern contact.

FIGURE 7.6
Evidence for granite emplacement by ballooning. A pure flattening fabric is displayed by quartz ribbons in the marginal granite at the northern contact of the Galway-Kilkieran Pluton. White broken lines indicate the strike of this subvertical quartz ribbon fabric (Glentrasna; 53.405643°, −9.541679°). See Graham (1997) and Baxter *et al.* (2005).

FIGURE 7.7
Arrested stoped blocks of dark grey country rocks belonging to the ~470 Ma Metagabbro Gneiss Suite and ranging up to 50 × 100 m, have been broken up and invaded by the light grey coloured granite veins (Feely *et al.*, 2006) (northern contact of the Galway-Kilkieran Pluton, Letterard; 53.363537°, −9.879136°).

References

Archibald, D.B., Macquarrie, L.M.G., Murphy, J.B., Strachan, R.A., McFarlane, C.R.M., Button, M., Larson, K.P. and Dunlop, J. 2021. The Construction of the Donegal Composite Batholith, Irish Caledonides: Temporal Constraints from U-Pb Dating of Zircon and Titanite. *GSA Bulletin*, 133(11–12), 2335–354.

Archibald, D.B. and Murphy, J.B. 2021. A Slab Failure Origin for the Donegal Composite Batholith, Ireland as Indicated by Trace-Element Geochemistry. In: B. Murphy, R.A. Strachan and C. Quesada (eds.) *Geological Society, London, Special Publications 503*, Pannotia to Pangaea: Neoproterozoic and Paleozoic Orogenic Cycles in the Circum-Atlantic Region. Geological Society, Burlington House, Piccadilly, London, 347–70.

Atherton, M.P. and Ghani, A.A. 2002. Slab Breakoff: A Model for Caledonian, Late Granite Syn-Collisional Magmatism in the Orthotectonic (Metamorphic) Zone of Scotland and Donegal, Ireland. *Lithos*, 62, 65–85.

Baxter, S. and Feely, M. 2002. Magma Mixing and Mingling Textures in Granitoids: Examples from the Galway Granite, Connemara, Ireland. *Mineralogy and Petrology*, 76, 63–7.

Baxter, S., Graham, N.T., Feely, M., Reavy, R.J. and Dewey, J.F. 2005. Fabric Studies of the Galway Granite, Connemara, Ireland. *Geological Magazine*, 142, 81–95.

Brown, P.E., Ryan, P. D., Soper, N.J. and Woodcock, N.H. 2008. The Newer Granite Problem Revisited: A Transtensional Origin for the Early Devonian Trans-Suture Suite. *Geological Magazine*, 145, 235–56.

Buchwaldt, R., Kroner, A., Toulkeredes, T., Todt, W. and Feely, M. 2001. Geochronology and Nd-Sr Systematics of Late Caledonian Granites in Western Ireland: New Implications for the Caledonian Orogeny. *Geological Society of America*, 33, 1, A32.

Chew, D.M. and Strachan, R.A. 2014. The Laurentian Caledonides of Scotland and Ireland. In: F. Corfu, D. Gasser and D.M. Chew (eds.) *New Perspectives on the Caledonides of Scandinavia and Related Areas*. Geological Society, London, Special Publications, vol. 390. Geological Society, Burlington House, Piccadilly, London, ISBN Print 9781862393776

Crowley, Q. and Feely, M. 1997. New Perspectives on the Order and Style of Granite Emplacement in the Galway Batholith, Western Ireland. *Geological Magazine*, 134, 539–48.

Dewey, J.F., Holdsworth, R.E. and Strachan, R.A. 1998. Transpression and Transtension Zones. In: R.E. Holdsworth, R.A. Strachan and J.F. Dewey (eds.) *Continental Transpressional and Transtensional Tectonics*. Geological Society, London, Special Publications, vol. 135, Geological Society, Burlington House, Piccadilly, London, 1–14.

Dewey, J.F. and Strachan, R.A. 2003. Changing Silurian-Devonian Relative Plate Motion in the Caledonides: Sinistral Transpression to Sinistral Transtension. *Journal of the Geological Society of London*, 160, 219–29.

Domeier, M. 2016. A Plate Tectonic Scenario for the Iapetus and Rheic Oceans. *Gondwana Research*, 36, 275–95.

El Desouky, M., Feely, M. and Mohr, P. 1996. Diorite-Granite Magma Mingling and Mixing Along the Axis of the Galway Granite Batholith, Ireland. *Journal of the Geological Society of London*, 153, 361–74.

Feely, M., Coleman, D., Baxter, S. and Miller, B. 2003. U-Pb Zircon Geochronology of the Galway Granite, Connemara, Ireland: Implications for the Timing of Late Caledonian Tectonic and Magmatic Events and for Correlations with Acadian Plutonism in New England. *Atlantic Geology*, 39, 175–84.

Feely, M., Gaynor, S., Venugopal, N., Hunt, J. and Coleman, D.S. 2018. New U-Pb Zircon Ages for the Inish Granite Pluton, Galway Granite Complex, Connemara, Western Ireland. *Irish Journal of Earth Sciences*, 36(1), 1–7.

Feely, M., Leake, B., Baxter, S., Hunt, J. and Mohr, P. 2006. *A Geological Guide to the Granites of the Galway Batholith, Connemara, Western Ireland*. Geological Survey of Ireland, Field guides Series. Geological Survey of Ireland, Dublin, 70p. ISBN 1-899702-56-3.

Feely, M., McCarthy, W., Costanzo, A., Leake, B.E.L. and Yardley, B.W.D. 2022. The Late Silurian to Upper Devonian Galway Granite Complex. In: P.D. Ryan (ed.) *A Field Guide to the Geology of Western Ireland*. Springer Geology Field Guides. Springer Nature, Switzerland, 303–62. Print ISBN 978-3-030-97478-7

Feely, M., Selby, D., Hunt, J. and Conliffe, J., 2010. Long-Lived Granite-Related Molybdenite Mineralization at Connemara, Western Irish Caledonides. *Geological Magazine*, 147(6), 886–94.

Graham, N.T. 1997. Fabric Studies in the Galway Granite, Ireland. PhD thesis, Oxford University. UK.

Leake, B.E. 1978. Granite Emplacement: The Granites of Ireland and Their Origin. In: D.R. Bowes and B.E. Leake (eds.) *Crustal Evolution in Northwest Britain and Adjacent Regions. Geol J.* 10, 221–48.

Leake, B.E. 2006. Mechanism of Emplacement and Crystallization History of the Northern Margin and Centre of the Galway Granite, Western Ireland. *Transactions of the Royal Society of Edinburgh: Earth Sciences*, 97, 1–23.

Leake, B.E. 2021. The Geology of the Clifden District, Connemara Co. Galway, Ireland, and Present Understanding of Connemara Geology. *Irish Journal of Earth Sciences*, 39, 1–28.

Leake, B.E. and Tanner, P.W.G. 1994. *The Geology of the Dalradian and Associated Rocks of Connemara, Western Ireland*. Royal Irish Academy. 96p. ISBN 1-874045-18-6.

Lees, A. and Feely, M. 2016. The Connemara Eastern Boundary Fault: A Review and Assessment Using New Evidence. *Irish Journal of Earth Sciences*, 34, 1–25.

Lees, A. and Feely, M. 2017. The Connemara Eastern Boundary Fault: A Correction. *Irish Journal of Earth Sciences*, 35, 55–6.

McCarthy, W. 2013. An Evaluation of Orogenic Kinematic Evolution Utilizing Crystalline and Magnetic Anisotropy in Granitoids. *PhD thesis, University College Cork, National University of Ireland*.

McCarthy, W., Petronis, M.S., Reavy, R.J. and Stevenson, C.T. 2015a. Distinguishing Diapirs from Inflated Plutons: An Integrated Rock Magnetic Fabric and Structural Study on the Roundstone Pluton, Western Ireland. *Journal of the Geological Society of London*, 172, 550–65.

McCarthy, W., Reavy, R.J., Stevenson, C.T. and Petronis, S. 2015b. Late Caledonian Transpression and the Structural Controls on Pluton Construction; New Insights from the Omey Pluton, Western Ireland. *Earth and Environmental Science Transactions of the Royal Society of Edinburgh*, 106(1), 11–28.

Miles, A.J., Woodcock, N.H. and Hawkesworth, C.J. 2016. Tectonic Controls on Post-Subduction Granite Genesis and Emplacement: The Late Caledonian Suite of Britain and Ireland. *Gondwana Research*, 39, 250–60.

Neilson, J.C., Kokelaar, B.P. and Crowley, Q.G. 2009. Timing, Relations and Cause of Plutonic and Volcanic Activity of the Siluro-Devonian Post-Collision Magmatic Episode in the Grampian Terrane, Scotland. *Journal of the Geological Society of London*, 166, 545–61.

van Staal, C.R., Whalen, J.B., Valverde-Vaquero, P., Zagorevski, A. and Rogers, N. 2009. Pre-Carboniferous, Episodic Accretion-Related, Orogenesis Along the Laurentian Margin of the Northern Appalachians. In: J.B. Murphy, J.D. Keppie and A.J. Hynes (eds.) *Ancient Orogens and Modern Analogues*. Geological Society, London, Special Publications, vol. 327, Geological Society, Burlington House, Piccadilly London, 271–16.

Wilson, R.A., van Staal, C.R. and Kamo, S.L. 2017. Rapid Transition from the Salinic to Acadian Orogenic Cycles in the Northern Appalachian Orogen: Evidence from Northern New Brunswick, Canada. *American Journal of Science*, 317, 449–82.

Woodcock, N.H., Soper, N.J. and Miles, A.J. 2019. Age of the Acadian Deformation and Devonian Granites in Northern England: A Review. *Proceedings of the Yorkshire Geological Society*, 62, 238–53.

Woodcock, N.H., Soper, N.J. and Strachan, R.A. 2007. A Rheic Cause for the Acadian Deformation in Europe. *Journal of the Geological Society, London*, 164, 1023–36.

8

The Plutons of the GGC: Emplacement, Field Relationships, Mineralogy and Petrology

The geology of the four Earlier Plutons and the plutons of the Galway Batholith (Carna and Galway-Kilkieran Plutons) is outlined. Detailed geological maps of each pluton are integrated with field examples and descriptions of their inter- and intra-granite relationships. The Earlier Plutons were emplaced into the rocks of the Connemara Metamorphic Complex. Inter- and intra-granite variations in mineral compositions for each pluton are plotted onto a QAP diagram. The Roundstone and Letterfrack plutons plot in the granodiorite field, whereas the Omey and Inish plutons plot in the granite field. The Carna Pluton is a ring complex composed of six granite varieties (Ards, Carna, Cuilleen, Errisbeg Townland and Murvey and Garnetiferous Murvey Granites) and the Galway-Kilkieran Pluton has nine granite types (Marginal Porphyritic, Megacrystic, Mafic Megacrystic, Mingling Mixing Zone, Lough Lurgan, Knock, Murvey, Shannapheasteen and the Costelloe Murvey Granites). QAP diagrams show that the granites of the Carna Pluton range in composition from granodiorites through granites to alkali feldspar granite (i.e., Murvey Granite). The granites of the Galway-Kilkieran pluton range from diorites and quartz diorites granodiorites to alkali feldspar granites. A temporal emplacement model for the large Galway-Kilkieran Pluton is used to account for the distribution of its individual granites.

The Earlier Plutons

The Earlier Plutons were emplaced into the rocks of the Connemara Metamorphic Complex. Inter- and intra-granite variations in mineral compositions for each pluton are displayed in Figure 8.1. The Roundstone and Letterfrack plutons plot in the granodiorite field, whereas the Omey and Inish plutons plot in the granite field. The geological setting of each pluton and the mineral compositions of each granite type are presented below.

DOI: 10.1201/9781032698410-8

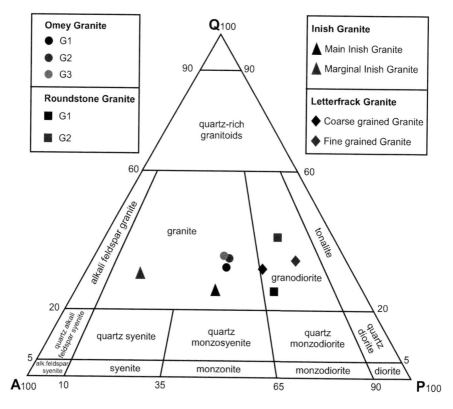

FIGURE 8.1

QAP ternary diagram for plutonic igneous rocks (Streckeisen, 1976) showing inter- and intra-granite variations in the Earlier Pluton suite. The granites of the Roundstone and Letterfrack Plutons plot in the granodiorite field in contrast with the granites of the Omey and Inish Plutons that plot in the granite field. QAP data for Omey Pluton from McCarthy (2015b); QAP data for the Inish Pluton from Townend (1966) and Leake (1986); QAP data for the Roundstone Pluton from McCarthy *et al.* (2015a); QAP data for the Letterfrack Pluton from Townend (1966).

The Omey Pluton

The Omey Pluton intruded the rocks belonging to the Streamstown Schist Formation and the Lakes Marble Formation at ~422 Ma (Feely *et al.*, 2007). The Pluton has a circular outcrop pattern and is ~6 km in diameter (Figure 8.2).

Coastal exposures SE of Fountain Hill reveal a granite country rock interface marked by thin sheets of chilled, fine-grained granite intruded into psammitic and pelitic hornfelses belonging to the Streamstown Schist Formation (Figure 8.3a). The latter are andalusite-bearing (Figure 8.3b). The granite sheets are concordant with the laminations in the hornfelses and reflect granite emplacement by stoping of the country rock. The contact zone is also

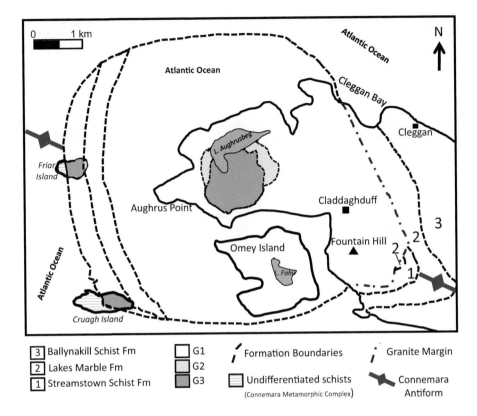

FIGURE 8.2
A geological map of the Omey Pluton and its Dalradian country rocks (after McCarthy *et al.*, 2015b). Broken lines are inferred geological contact.

marked by the presence of discordant sheets of very fine-grained white to pink aplite.

The pluton consists of three main granite types: G1, G2 and G3. The G1 granite accounts for ~75% of the surface area of the pluton (Figure 8.2). It is a medium-grained (~8 mm) equigranular, biotite+hornblende granite with alkali feldspar (30%), oligoclase-andesine (34%), quartz (30%), biotite (3%) and hornblende (~2%). G2 is exposed between G1 and G3 and is a medium-grained biotite + hornblende granite similar to G1. It is composed of potassium-feldspar (29%), andesine (33%), quartz (34%), biotite (3%) and hornblende (<1%). G2 locally contains potassium-feldspar megacrysts (~4 cm in longest dimension). G3 forms a small circular intrusion (diameter ~1.2 km) that is exposed on the Aughrus Peninsula (Figure 8.2). It is a fine- to medium-grained (~2–6 mm) pink granite containing potassium-feldspar (30%), oligoclase (32%), quartz (35%), biotite (2%) and muscovite (~1%). The G3 is recognised in the field by a porphyritic texture defined by ~15 mm

FIGURE 8.3
(a) Contact zone of the Omey G1 granite with the laminated pelites of the Streamstown Schist
Fm. The pink fine-grained granite sheets parallel the laminations/bedding in the country rocks
(beach SE of Fountain Hill; 53.528613°, −10.138298°). (b) Andalusite hornfels (Streamstown
Schist Formation) within the aureole of the Omey Pluton. The diameter of the coin is 2.5 cm
(beach SE of Fountain Hill; 53.527749°, −10.137207°).

long plagioclase and orthoclase feldspars phenocrysts and ~12 mm anhedral to rounded quartz grains. All the granite types contain accessory minerals (~1%) that include zircon, rutile and apatite. The QAP ternary diagram (Figure 8.1) shows that G1, G2 and G3 all plot within the granite field.

The pluton was emplaced into the southeasterly plunging (~25°) hinge region of the D4 Connemara antiform by a combination of centrally focused magma ascent and lateral emplacement of G1 followed by G2 and finally by G3. The emplacement was controlled by the symmetry of the Connemara antiform, forming a convex upwards lens-shaped igneous intrusion (mushroom shaped) called a phacolith (McCarthy *et al.*, 2015b).

The thermal metamorphic history of the Pluton's aureole rocks has been well documented by Cobbing (1969), Ferguson and Harvey (1979), Ferguson and Al-Ameen (1985). Detailed field descriptions of the aureole rocks were also presented by Feely *et al.* (2022). Pelites and carbonates of the Streamstown Schist and Lakes Marble Formations display contact metamorphic lithologies including andalusite hornfelses and wollastonite-grossular garnet-vesuvianite (idocrase)-diopside skarns. Andalusite and cordierite occur up to 1.4 km, and thermal biotite up to 2 km from the granite contact (Leake and Tanner, 1994). Ferguson and Al-Ameen (1985) calculated the inner aureole P-T conditions at 615 ± 25°C and 2.5 ± 0.25 kbar.

The Inish Pluton

The Inish Pluton intruded the rocks of the Metagabbro Gneiss Suite and the Dalradian metasediments (Bennabeola Quartzite Formation and Streamstown Schist Formation) at ~423 Ma. (Feely *et al.*, 2018). Only its northern and eastern edges are exposed, the former on the islands of Inishturk and Turbot, and the latter along the western shoreline of Errismore peninsula (Figure 8.4). The pluton comprises two granite varieties: the Main Inish Granite and a marginal, finer-grained variety called the Marginal Granite. Locally, the Marginal Granite was intruded into by the Main Inish Granite (Leake, 1986).

Geochronology studies by Feely *et al.* (2018) show that the earlier Marginal Granite was emplaced at 423.77 ± 0.26 Ma and the younger Main Inish Granite was emplaced at 422.72 ± 0.19 Ma. The Main Inish Granite is equigranular (2–8 mm) composed of plagioclase feldspar (~30%), microcline+microperthite (~30%), quartz (~20%), biotite (~7–10%), hornblende (~1–5%) and accessory zircon and apatite. The Marginal Granite is finer-grained (1–2 mm) and is composed of microcline-microperthite (~40–45%), quartz (~20–25%), plagioclase feldspar (~10%), hornblende (~10%), biotite (~1%) and accessory zircon and apatite. The Main Inish Granite and the Marginal Granite plot in the granite field of the QAP ternary diagram (Figure 8.1).

The marginal zone granite contains many disoriented stoped blocks of the country rocks and passes outwards into a zone marked by a concentration of potassium-feldspar -rich aplopegmatite veins that cut the country rocks.

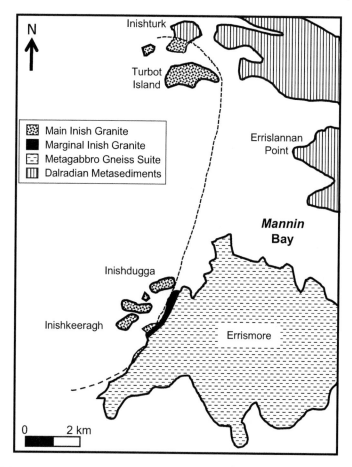

FIGURE 8.4

Geological map of Inish Pluton after Townend (1966) and Leake (1986). Broken lines are inferred geological contact.

NE trending D3 folds in the country rocks tighten towards the granite margin reflecting the push by the intruding granite magma to make room for its emplacement (Leake, 1986). Andalusite-bearing pelitic hornfelses occur in the aureole rocks (Leake, 1986).

The Roundstone Pluton

The Roundstone Pluton has a circular-shaped outcrop pattern with a diameter of ~8 km, and it was intruded into the Metagabbro Gneiss Suite. The Roundstone Pluton has yielded a U-Pb zircon age of c. 420 Ma (McCarthy, 2013; McCarthy *et al.*, 2015a). In addition, Friedrich and Hodges (2016) reported an $^{40}Ar/^{39}Ar$ biotite age of 420 ± 4 Ma from the Roundstone Pluton.

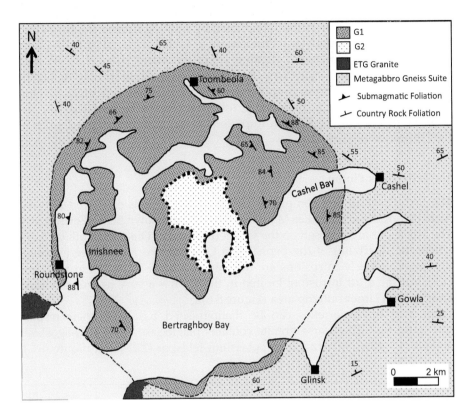

FIGURE 8.5
The geology of the Roundstone Pluton and its country rocks (the Metagabbro Gneiss Suite). Contact parallel planar fabrics are also shown. After McCarthy *et al.*, 2015a. Broken lines are inferred geological contact. Abbreviations: ETG: Errisbeg Townland Granite.

The pluton consists of two granite varieties, G1 and G2 (Figure 8.5). G1 represents the major component of the intrusion, and G2 occurs as a network of steeply dipping NNW–SSE striking sheets that transect G1 near the core of the intrusion. Gradational and lobate contacts between G1 and G2 and no intergranite chilled margins indicate that the emplacement of these two granite types was coeval. G1 is equigranular and contains biotite, hornblende (2–5 mm grain size) and euhedral to subhedral plagioclase feldspar and potassium feldspar phenocrysts. It contains plagioclase feldspar (~47%), quartz (23%), potassium feldspar (21%), biotite (7%), hornblende (1%) and accessory minerals (1%), e.g., zircon and apatite. G2 is finer-grained (0.5–2 mm) and equigranular, containing plagioclase feldspar (42%), quartz (39%), potassium feldspar (13%), biotite (5%) and accessory minerals (1%), e.g., zircon and apatite. These two varieties plot in the granodiorite field of the QAP ternary diagram (Figure 8.1).

As noted in Chapter 7, the role played by faulting during the formation of the Omey and Roundstone Plutons suggests that regional sinistral transpression at ~420 Ma caused dilation along the intersection of NNW–SSE and ENE–WSW fault structures. This facilitated centralised magma ascent to form these two plutons. Emplacement by a combination of block stoping and pluton inflation, i.e., ballooning, followed (McCarthy *et al.*, 2015a). The latter emplacement mechanism imparted contact parallel planar fabrics in the G1 granite (Figure 8.5).

The Letterfrack Pluton

The Letterfrack Pluton comprises three small intrusions emplaced into the rocks belonging to the Lakes Marble and the Streamstown Schist Formations. The intrusions are exposed on the southern slopes of Diamond Hill (0.4 km), where the quartzites of the Bennabeola Quartzite Formation are exposed. The more westerly intrusions are roughly circular (~0.5–0.75 km in diameter), but the third intrusion, located in the SE, has a very irregular outline and covers a larger outcrop area (Figure 8.6).

The two main varieties can be distinguished based on their respective grain size. The coarse granite contains plagioclase feldspar (oligoclase-andesine) (~45%), quartz (30%), potassium-feldspar (22%) and biotite (8%).

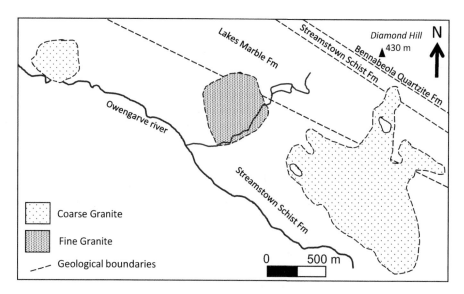

FIGURE 8.6
Geological map of the Letterfrack Pluton and its country rocks.

(Modified after Townend, 1966 and Leake and Tanner, 1994.)

The finer-grained granite has less potassium-feldspar (10%) and forms the middle intrusion. Both varieties plot in the granodiorite field of the QAP ternary diagram (Figure 8.1). They display a grey, equigranular appearance, quite distinct from the pink porphyritic granites of the other early plutons, i.e., Omey and Roundstone Plutons. The shallow outward dips of the contacts indicate that the three individual intrusions are part of one large pluton. Large, stoped blocks of country rocks belonging to the Streamstown Schist and Lakes Marble Formations are present in the larger southeastern intrusion.

The Galway Batholith

The Galway Batholith consists of two plutons: the Carna Pluton (~410 Ma) and the Galway-Kilkieran Pluton (~400 Ma). Both are composite plutons; the Carna Pluton is composed of six granite varieties while the Galway-Kilkieran Pluton has nine granite types.

The Carna Pluton

The Carna Pluton comprises the central Mace-Ards Granite surrounded by the Carna and Cuilleen granites. The latter granite occurs as a sheet within the more dominant Carna Granite (Figure 8.7). The dominant Carna Granite is aphyric and has quartz (~24%), potassium feldspar (24%), plagioclase feldspar (42%), biotite (7%), hornblende (2%) and accessory minerals (~1%), e.g., titanite and apatite. The Cuilleen Granite is a potassium feldspar porphyry composed of quartz (~27%), potassium feldspar (23%), plagioclase feldspar (43%), biotite (5%), and accessory minerals (~1%), e.g., hornblende, sphene and apatite. The Carna and Cuilleen varieties plot in both the granite and granodiorite fields close to the granite-granodiorite boundary in the QAP ternary diagram (Figure 8.8).

The Errisbeg Townland Granite (ETG) displays a sharp intrusive contact with the country rocks belonging to the Metagabbro Gneiss Suite (MMGS) of the Connemara Metamorphic Complex (Figure 8.9a). It is a coarse-grained pink phenocrystic granite (Figure 8.9b) composed of quartz (~29%), potassium feldspar (31%), plagioclase feldspar (34%), biotite (5%) and accessories (1%), e.g., hornblende, sphene. It plots in the granite field on the QAP diagram (Figure 8.8).

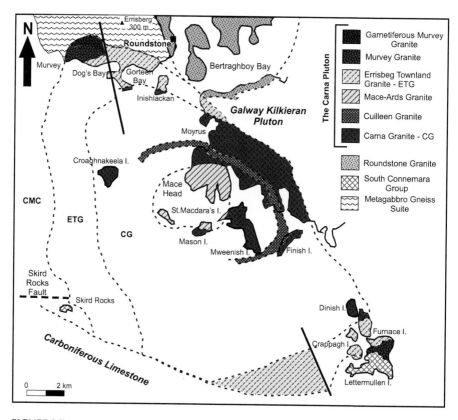

FIGURE 8.7
The geology of the Carna Pluton adapted from Wright (1964), Max *et al.* (1978) and Leake (2011). Abbreviations: Connemara Metamorphic Complex (CMC), Errisbeg Townland Granite (ETG), Carna Granite (CG). Broken lines are inferred geological contact.

The Carna Granite displays a gradational contact (<200 m wide) with the surrounding marginal potassium feldspar porphyritic ETG. The contact is defined by a gradual southward decrease in size and abundance of pink potassium feldspar phenocrysts towards the centrally located Carna Granite, SW of Gorteen Bay (Figure 8.7). The arcuate Gorteen Bay and Dog's Bay form a tombolo (Figure 8.10). Dog's Bay is noteworthy for its foraminiferal sands. The foraminifera shells (<1 mm across) can account for 60% of the beach sand (Murray, 2009). The foraminifera enter Dog's Bay, become trapped and form these beach sand deposits.

The narrow beach along the shore, ~200 m west of Dog's Bay, is where the Cleggan–Clifden–Dog's Bay Fault crosses the bay (Figure 8.10) and played a key role during the emplacement of the Galway Granite Complex (see Chapter 7).

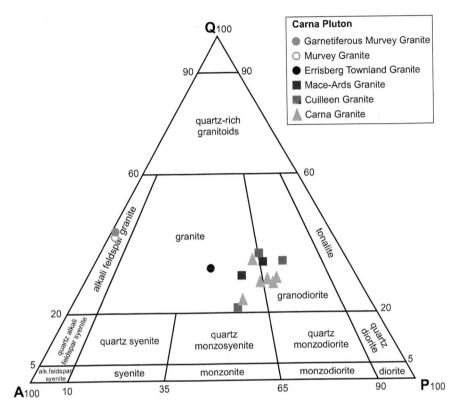

FIGURE 8.8

QAP ternary diagram for plutonic igneous rocks (Streckeisen, 1976) showing the inter-and intra-granite variations displayed by the granites of the Carna Pluton. The diagram shows the Carna Pluton rocks range in composition from granodiorites through granites to alkali feldspar granite (i.e., Murvey Granite). The Carna, Cuilleen and Mace-Ards Granites straddle the granodiorite-granite fields. Data from Wright (1964), Leake (1974) and Leake (2011).

A similar gradational contact is exposed further to the southeast on Furnace Island in the South Connemara archipelago (Figure 8.7). Proceeding southwards the granite composition gradually changes from the Carna Granite through a transitional zone to the ETG and finally to the leucocratic marginal Murvey Granite in contact with the rocks of the South Connemara Group-see Feely *et al.*, 2006 for a detailed map of this transition zone. These gradational contacts indicate that both granite magmas were essentially coeval and crystallised side by side without the formation of a sharp intrusive chilled boundary (Leake, 1974).

The southern margin of the Carna Pluton is exposed on Crappagh Island (Figure 8.7) where the ETG chills against the basic volcanics of the South Connemara Group (Ryan and Feely, 1983; Feely *et al.*, 2006). The granite displays a centimetric chilled margin that can be followed westwards for ~500 m.

FIGURE 8.9

(a) Contact between the ETG and the MGGS of the Connemara Metamorphic Complex (looking north from Dog's Bay, west of Roundstone; 53.378030°, −9.963147°). (b) Exposure of ETG, N of Dog's Bay, displaying typical salmon pink potassium feldspars phenocrysts set in a finer-grained groundmass composed of quartz, milky white plagioclase (oligoclase) and flecks of biotite (53.385791°, −9.972679°). (c) Igneous layering in the ETG, W of Dog's Bay, layers here dip to the N at ~20° (53.383335°, −9.969736°).

On Lettermullan Island cordierite ± andalusite hornfelses are commonly displayed by the pelitic metasediments in the South Connemara Group (Ryan and Dewey, 2022).

Igneous layering is a common feature of the ETG (Figure 8.9c). Alternating layers (10 cm to 2 m thick) are biotite-rich or potassium feldspar-rich and were formed by gravity settling before the ETG magma fully crystallised (Leake, 1974). The layers dip at angles of ~20° outwards from the central Carna Granite. The outward dipping mineral layering indicates that the layers were pushed upwards by the central intrusion of the Carna Granite.

FIGURE 8.10
Looking to the southeast onto Dog's Bay and Gorteen Bay that together form a Tombolo (a sandy or shingle isthmus). The narrow beach ~200 m west of Dog's Bay marks the trace of the major Cleggan-Clifden-Dog's Bay Fault.

A leucocratic alkali-feldspar granite, the Murvey Granite, occurs between the ETG and the country rocks belonging to the MGGS. The Murvey Granite contains quartz (~34%), potassium feldspar (34%), albite (30%), biotite (2%) and accessory magnetite. A sharp contact between these two granites is visible on some exposures (Figure 8.11). Field relationships indicate that the latter granite type crystallised above the ETG.

A fine-grained garnetiferous Murvey Granite (Leake, 1968; Whitworth and Feely, 1994) is present west of Roundstone at the NW contact with the country rock (Figure 8.7). Chronometric data (Table 8.1) supports the field relationships and confirms that the Murvey Granite (and by inference the ETG) formed at ~410 Ma and were intruded by the slightly younger, but still crystallising, Carna Granite at ~407 Ma.

At Mace Head, west of Carna, a felsic granite with 5% modal biotite + muscovite called the Mace-Ards granite intrudes the Carna granite (Leake, 2011; Figure 8.7). This granite plots close to the granodiorite-granite boundary on the QAP ternary diagram (Figure 8.8). Southeast of Mace Head (within the Mace Ards Granite), orbicular structures occur, consisting of dark grey cores 40–70 mm in diameter, with pale granite margins (10–40 mm wide) (Figure 8.12). The orbicule cores contain quartz and cordierite; the latter is heavily replaced by muscovite. The orbicular granite is spatially related to the Mace Head

FIGURE 8.11
Sharp contact between the Murvey Granite and the ETG (north of Dog's Bay; 53.383538°, −9.982526°).

TABLE 8.1

Chronometric data from the Carna Pluton

CARNA PLUTON	
Zircon (bulk sample) (U-Pb)	Molybdenite in Murvey Granite Hosted Quartz Vein (Re-Os)
[1]Carna Gr.	[2]Carna Gr.
412 ± 15 Ma	(Mace Head)
	407.3 ± 1.5 Ma
	[2]Marginal Murvey Gr.
	(W of Roundstone)
	410.5 ± 1.5 Ma
	and 410.8 ± 1.4 Ma

Data from [1] Pidgeon (1969) and [2] Selby *et al.* (2004).

Mo-Cu mineralisation, which includes disseminated and quartz vein-hosted molybdenite and chalcopyrite mineralisation, a potassium-feldspar breccia, and quartz-magnetite pods. All these features are described and illustrated in Chapter 9.

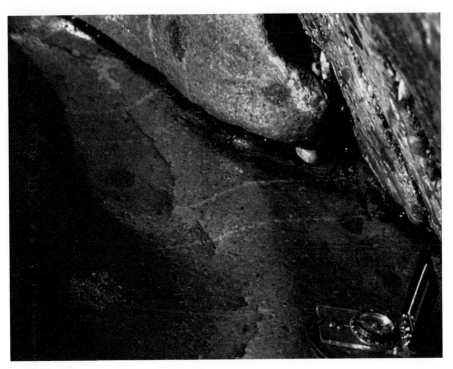

FIGURE 8.12
Orbicular granite from the Mace Ards Granite. Note the dark cores containing cordierite and quartz and the leucocratic granite margins (53.315967°, −9.886721°). Edge of compass clinometer is 10 cm in length.

Feldspar Compositions in the Carna Pluton

Potassium feldspar and plagioclase compositions for the granites of the Carna Pluton have been reported by Leake (1974 and 2011) as follows: 1) the Murvey Granite has potassium feldspar ($\sim Or_{93-97}$) and plagioclase ($\sim An_{13-8}$); 2) the Garnetiferous Murvey Granite has plagioclase ($\sim An_2$) and perthite ($\sim Or_{94}$); 3) in both the ETG and the Carna Granite the potassium feldspar is perthitic ($\sim Or_{85-97}$) and plagioclase is normally zoned ($\sim An_{35-15}$); 4) the Cuilleen Granite has normally zoned plagioclase ($\sim An_{31-19}$) and potassium feldspar ($\sim Or_{90}$); 5) the Mace Ards Granite has normally zoned plagioclase ($\sim An_{40-17}$) and potassium feldspar ($\sim Or_{86-97}$). Wright (1964) noted that the potassium feldspar in the Carna Pluton is intermediate in structure between microcline perthite and orthoclase perthite.

The Galway-Kilkieran Pluton

The Galway-Kilkieran Pluton (GKP) is the largest pluton in the Galway Granite Complex. It is cut by the NNE-trending Shannawona Fault and the NW-trending Barna Fault (Figure 8.13). These two faults create three fault blocks, i.e., the western, central and eastern blocks. They control the overall distribution of the granite types in the GKP. Some of the central block granites display deformation-related fabrics, aligned discoidal mafic microgranular enclaves and magma mingling textures. These foliated and mafic granodiorites, e.g., Mafic Megacrystic Granodiorite (MMGr) and Mingling Mixing Zone Granodiorite (MMZGr) were intruded by unfoliated granites, e.g., Costelloe

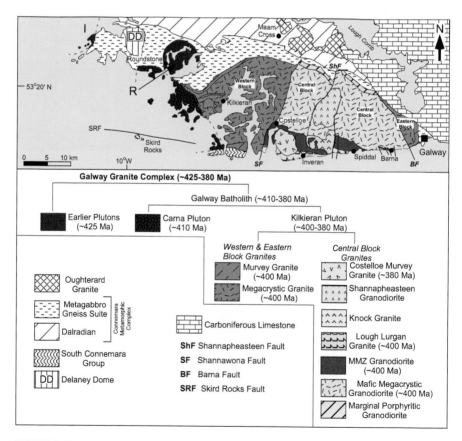

FIGURE 8.13

Geological map of the Galway-Kilkieran Pluton adapted from Coats and Wilson (1971), Max *et al.* (1978), Leake *et al.* (1981), Leake and Tanner (1994), El-Desouky *et al.* (1996), Crowley and Feely (1997), Baxter and Feely (2002), Baxter *et al.* (2005), Callaghan (2005), Leake (2006) and Leake (2011). The Galway Granite Complex is divided into its component granite units. R and I indicate the location of the Earlier Plutons, i.e., Roundstone and Inish Plutons.

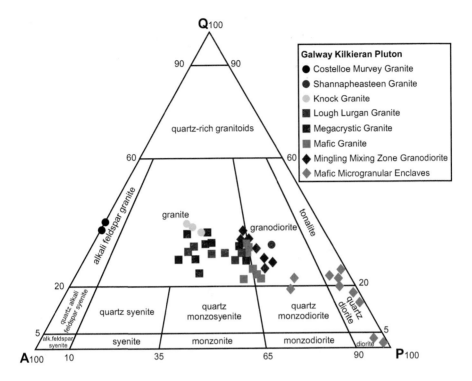

FIGURE 8.14
QAP ternary diagram for plutonic igneous rocks (Streckeisen, 1976) showing the range of granite compositions that comprise the G-KP. Modal data from: El-Desouky *et al.* (1996), Crowley and Feely (1997) and Leake (2006).

Murvey Granite and the Shannapheasteen Granodiorite (Figure 8.13). The central block reveals magmatic processes that were active during the ascent and emplacement of the GKP (Baxter and Feely 2002; Baxter *et al.*, 2005). The QAP ternary diagram (Figure 8.14) shows that the granite types encountered in the GKP range in composition from diorite and quartz diorite enclaves to granodiorites, granites and alkali feldspar granites (Feely *et al.*, 2006). Furthermore, the QAP diagram shows that the granites of the western and eastern blocks plot in the granite field in contrast with the wide compositional range of granite types, i.e., from diorite to granodiorite and granite to alkali feldspar granite exposed in the central block. The potassium-feldspar (KAlSi$_3$O$_8$) in the GKP can be either orthoclase or microcline (Leake, 2006). Coats and Wilson (1971) reported the presence of megacrysts of orthoclase microperthite in the Megacrystic Granite and microcline megacrysts in the Mafic Megacrystic Granodiorite. Plagioclase feldspar compositions for the range of granites in the GKP are presented in Table 8.2. Geochronometry reveals that most of the granites comprising the GKP were intruded at ~ 400 Ma (Table 8.3), in marked contrast, to ~410 Ma age of the Carna Pluton granites (Table 8.1).

TABLE 8.2

Plagioclase feldspar compositions for the granites (mafic microgranular enclaves are also included) of the Galway-Kilkieran Pluton

GALWAY-KILKIERAN PLUTON

Granite type	Plagioclase
Western and Eastern Blocks	
Megacrystic Granite	An_{25-10}
Murvey Granite	An_{14-6}
Central Block	
Mafic Microgranular Enclaves	An_{45-35}
Mafic Megacrystic Granodiorite	An_{33-20}
Mingling Mixing Zone Granodiorite	An_{32-28}
Lough Lurgan Granite	An_{30-11}
Knock Granite	An_{32-27}
Costelloe Murvey Granite	An_{5-2}

Data Sources: Wright, 1964; Coats and Wilson, 1971; Feely, 1982; El Desouky *et al.*, 1996; Crowley and Feely, 1997; Leake, 2006.

TABLE 8.3

Geochronology of the Galway-Kilkieran Pluton

Galway Kilkieran Pluton	Zircon Single Crystal (U-Pb)	Molybdenite in Vein Quartz (Re-Os)	Biotite in Granite Ar/Ar
Western Block	Murvey Gr.[a] 402.2 ± 1.1 Ma		MegacrysticGr.[b] 402 ± 3 Ma
Central Block	Mafic Megacrystic Gr.[c] 394.4 ± 2.2 Ma	Lough Lurgan Gr.[a] 399.5 ± 1.7 Ma	
	Mafic Megacrystic Gr.[c] c. 402 Ma	Mafic Megacrystic Gr. 401.0 ± 0.2 Ma[d]	
	Mafic Megacrystic Gr.[d] 401.89 ± 0.33 Ma		
	Mafic Microgranular Enclave (MME)[c] 397.7 ± 1.1 Ma		
	Mingling Mixing Zone Gr.[c] 399.5 ± 0.8 Ma		
	Costelloe Murvey Gr[c] 380.1 ± 5.5 Ma		

Notes: The Geochronometric data is from:

[a] Feely *et al.* (2010).

[b] Friedrich and Hodges (2016).

[c] Feely *et al.* (2003).

[d] Feely *et al.* (2020).

The Granites of the Western and Eastern Blocks

The Western Block

The Megacrystic Granite and a medium to fine-grained leucogranite called the Murvey Granite occur in the western block (Figure 8.13). The latter occurs along the northern and southern margins of the western block (Figure 8.13). Two sheets like intrusions of the Murvey Granite also occur to the west of the village of Kilkieran (Figure 8.13) and yield a Re-Os age of ~402 Ma (Table 8.3). This Murvey Granite is similar in texture and mineralogy to the older ~410 Ma Murvey Granite of the Carna Pluton (Table 8.1).

The Megacrystic Granite (MGr) is a coarse-grained porphyritic granite containing salmon pink potassium feldspar (~Or_{95}) phenocryts (up to 8 cm long). The MGr yields a biotite Ar^{39}/Ar^{40} age of ~402 Ma (Friedrich and Hodges, 2016) – see Table 8.3. It is similar in texture and mineralogy to the older (~410 Ma) Errisbeg Townland Granite in the Carna Pluton. Geochronology supports the field observations of Wright (1964), who concluded that the MGr intruded the ~410 Ma Carna Pluton. Furthermore, Wright (1964) noted that the MGr and Murvey Granite contact is frequently sheared. However, locally, there is evidence of chilling in the Murvey Granite indicating that it intruded the MGr.

The Eastern Block

The MGr and the Murvey Granite also occur in the eastern fault block which forms part of the bedrock of Galway city (Figures 8.13 and 8.15). The Murvey Granite outcrops as a strip adjacent to the country rock (~470 Ma Metagabbro Gneiss Suite: MGGS). The Murvey Granite intruded the MGGS and the contact strikes roughly NS, perpendicular to the gneissic foliation in the gneisses (Coats and Wilson, 1971). The poorly exposed contact between the MGr and the Murvey Granite is gradational over ~1 metre. The former loses its potassium feldspar phenocrysts as the contact with the Murvey Granite is approached (Coats and Wilson, 1971). The boundary between the Carboniferous rocks and the basement rocks (i.e., the granite and its MGGS country rocks) is a faulted contact marked by the Connemara Eastern Boundary Fault (Lees and Feely, 2016 and 2017).

The bedrock of Galway's inner city belongs to the MGGS and its dark grey amphibolites and granite gneisses can be observed in many of the dry-stone walls in the inner part of the city, e.g., along the canal and opposite the Cathedral. The Gate-Lodge at the main entrance to the University of Galway is mainly built from the dark grey MGGS bedrock (Figure 8.16a)

The river Corrib cuts through the MGGS forming steep banks at the Salmon Weir Bridge. Proceeding westwards from the city centre to Salthill the bedrock geology abruptly changes from the MGGS to the Murvey

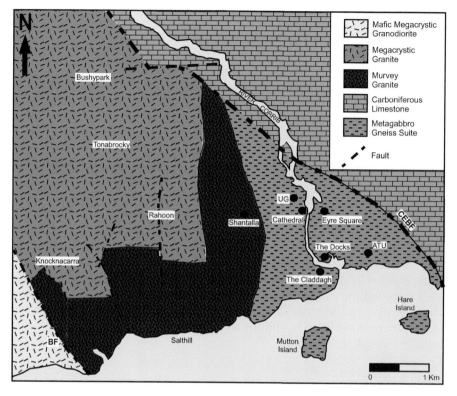

FIGURE 8.15
Map of the Eastern Block of the G-KP highlighting the distribution of bedrock types in Galway city. The Barna Fault (BF) marks the boundary between the Central Block and the Eastern Block. Abbreviations: CEBF: Connemara Eastern Boundary Fault; UG: University of Galway; ATU: Atlantic Technological University.

(Map adapted from Coats and Wilson, 1971 and Lees and Feely, 2016, 2017.)

Granite (Figure 8.15). The 19th-century Claddagh Dominican Church was largely built from locally quarried granite blocks and fashioned pillars of the Megacrystic Gr (Figure 8.16 b and c). Carboniferous limestone was used to construct many of the major mid-19th-century buildings in Galway including the University of Galway's Quadrangle Building and in Eyre Square most of the bank buildings, the railway station, and the adjoining hotel (The Hardiman). Arguably the last great building to be constructed of natural stone in Ireland is the 'Cathedral of Our Lady Assumed into Heaven and St Nicholas' that was opened in 1965 (Figure 8.16 d and inset).

FIGURE 8.16

(a) The gate-lodge of the University of Galway constructed of dark grey blocks of the MGGS and blocks of lighter grey local Carboniferous limestone. (b) The 19th-century Claddagh Dominican Church constructed of locally quarried pink granite blocks edged by Galway grey limestone blocks. (c) A close-up view of a load-bearing Megacrystic Granite pillar from the interior of the Claddagh Dominican Church. The salmon pink potassium feldspar phenocrysts are a characteristic of this granite type. (d) A fossiliferous limestone block used to build the Cathedral of Our Lady Assumed into Heaven and St Nicholas (inset). Blocks of this limestone were quarried to the east of the city, e.g., Angliham quarry, and from further east near Ballinasloe. See Feely *et al.* (2002) and Feely and Costanzo (2014).

(Images by Pat O'Connor at www.westerneyes-photography.com.)

The Granites of the Central Block

The central block exposes a wider range of granite types than those comprising the eastern and western blocks – see the QAP diagram (Figure 8.14). Seven major rock types occur in the central block: (1) the Marginal Porphyritic Granodiorite (MPGr), (2) the Mafic Megacrystic Granodiorite (MMGr), (3) the Mingling Mixing Zone Granodiorite (MMZGr), (4) the Lough Lurgan Granite (LLGr), (5) the Knock Granite (KGr), (6) the Shannapheasteen Granodiorite (ShGr) and (7) the Costelloe Murvey Granite (CMGr). Granite types 1 to 4 are foliated and granites 5 to 7 are unfoliated and intrude the foliated granites. A summary description of each granite type follows:

The Marginal Porphyritic Granodiorite (MPGr)

A marginal zone (500–700 m wide) of foliated potassium feldspar (<2 cm long) porphyritic granite called the Marginal Porphyritic Granodiorite (MPGr) occurs along the northern contact zone of the central block. The edge of the MPGr is conformable with the ESE strike and steep dip (~80°N) of the country rocks. The MPGr displays a gradational contact (~100 m) with the relatively coarse, foliated Mafic Megacrystic Granodiorite (MMGr).

The Mafic Megacrystic Granodiorite (MMGr)

The MMGr has salmon pink potassium feldspar (Or_{95} orthoclase or microcline megacrysts, ~5–10 cm long, typically ~5 cm). Crowley and Feely (1997) reported that the potassium feldspar megacrysts comprise equal proportions of orthoclase and perthite. The MPGr and MMGr contain quartz, zoned plagioclase (andesine and oligoclase), salmon pink orthoclase (some perthitic) or microcline, biotite and hornblende (~15% modal abundance), accessories include titanite, zircon and apatite (El Desouky *et al.*, 1996; Crowley and Feely 1997; Leake, 2006) (Figure 8.17). The MMGr contains aligned discoidal mafic microgranular enclaves (MME) that are <1 m in longest dimension. Alignments of the enclaves, potassium-feldspar megacrysts and groundmass minerals (e.g., hornblende and biotite) define a WNW trending fabric dipping steeply to NNE. This fabric becomes more prominent as the conformable intrusive contact with the MPGr is approached.

The Mingling Mixing Zone Granodiorite (MMZGr)

The MMZGr is ~ 3 to 4 km wide and extends for ~25 km from the coast at Spiddal to the Carraroe peninsula in the west, where it is cut by and terminates against the ENE trending Shannawona Fault (Figure 8.13). In the east, near Barna, a separate and narrower (<100 m wide) WNW trending mingling mixing zone occurs in the MMGr. It has a strike length of ~5 km, see details of the Barna mingling mixing zone in Baxter (2000), Baxter and Feely (2002) and Feely *et al.* (2006). El Desouky *et al.* (1996) reported that the medium

FIGURE 8.17
Polished sample of the MMGr displaying salmon pink potassium feldspars, milky white plagioclase (oligoclase) and hornblende prisms (Hbl).

to coarse-grained (1–10 mm) MMZGr comprises a hybrid granodiorite containing many mafic microgranular enclaves (MME). Varying degrees of mingling between the hybrid granodiorite and the MME can be observed from intensely stretched mafic enclaves to ovoid and spherical enclaves. The fabric in the MMZGr is defined by the alignment of discoidal MME (Figure 8.18a). Furthermore, the alignment of potassium feldspar, plagioclase (An_{45-27}), hornblende and biotite both in the host hybrid granodiorite and the enclaves accentuate the foliated nature of the MMZGr. The fabric dips to the north-northeast and steepens towards the contact with the MMGr in the north.

World-renowned coastal exposures of the MMZGr displaying abundant discoidal MME can be examined along the shoreline north of the Martello Tower at Rossaveel (Feely *et al.*, 2006, 2022). Magma-mingling textures are commonly displayed by the MME throughout the Spiddal to Carraroe zone and the Barna zone, e.g., titanite-plagioclase ocelli, quartz-hornblende ocelli, rapakivi feldspar, potassium feldspar megacrysts in MME and mafic clots of hornblende ± magnetite (~2 mm) both in the MME and in the hybrid host (Figure 8.18b; see more examples in: Baxter and Feely 2002 and Feely *et al.*, 2006). Titanite-plagioclase ocelli are commonly displayed by the MME along the shoreline north of the Martello Tower (Figure 8.19a).

FIGURE 8.18
(a) Blasted roadside exposure displaying the heterogeneous nature of the MMZGr. Costelloe road cutting (53.286552°, −9.545798°). (b) Photomicrograph (PPL) of the MMZGr displaying a clot of hornblende+magnetite crystals similar to the mafic clots encountered in the enclaves (see Figure 8.19b). Their ubiquitous presence in the MMZGr attests to the coeval mingling between the diorite and granite magmas. Abbreviations: quartz (Qz); potassium feldspar (Kfs); plagioclase feldspar (Pl, oligoclase-andesine); titanite (Ttn).

FIGURE 8.19
(a) Titanite-plagioclase ocelli hosted by an MME from the MMZGr. The cores of each ocelli contain clusters of titanite surrounded by plagioclase feldspar. Martello Tower shoreline (53.257156°, −9.563157°). (b) Photomicrograph (PPL) of an MME displaying a clot of hornblende prisms similar to the clot highlighted in Figure 8.18b. Abbreviations: quartz (Qz); potassium feldspar (Kfs); plagioclase feldspar (Pl, oligoclase-andesine), titanite (Ttn).

The Lough Lurgan Granite (LLGr)

The LLGr is a medium to coarse (1–7 mm)-grained granite with quartz (26%), orthoclase (28%), plagioclase (37%; An_{30}), biotite (~5%) and rare hornblende (<0.5%). Accessory minerals include titanite and apatite. The LLGr intrudes the MMZGr and its foliation is cut by the LLGr east of Spiddal and apophyses of the LLGr are seen within the MMZGr south of Costelloe (El Desouky *et al.*, 1996). SW-NE alignments of MME also occur in the LLGr.

The Knock Granite (KGr)

The KGr is a light pink, medium to coarse-grained granite with quartz (~34%), orthoclase (~34%), plagioclase (~25% An_{32-27}), biotite (~5%) and rare hornblende (<1%). Accessories include titanite and apatite. The granite has kilometre scale stoped blocks of the MMZGr. However, the KGr does not possess a foliation and modal hornblende is <1.0% (Crowley and Feely, 1997).

The Shannapheasteen Granodiorite (ShGr)

The Shannapheasteen Granodiorite (ShGr), NE of Spiddal, is a fine-grained (0.5–1.5 mm) granodiorite that intrudes the foliated MMGr and contains numerous stoped blocks of the latter while many veins of the ShG have injected the MMGr. It is generally hornblende-free, contains chloritised biotite, oligoclase and the potassium feldspar is either orthoclase or microcline (Leake, 2006).

The Costelloe Murvey Granite (CMGr)

The Costelloe Murvey Granite (CMGr) resembles the other leucogranites (i.e., Murvey Granites) mapped elsewhere in the Carna and Galway-Kilkieran plutons. The CMGr displays sharp intrusive contacts with the surrounding MMZGr and the LLGr.

The roughly circular surface exposure covers an area of ~30 km². Gravity studies indicate that CMGr intrusion has a maximum depth of ~3 km

FIGURE 8.20
The Costelloe Murvey Granite: (a) the pink leucocratic CMGr, (b) rare spessartine-bearing quartz microcline (amazonite) pegmatites, (c) horizontal and vertical joints in the roof zone of the CMGr and (d) dendritic hematite common on CMGr joints (Costelloe Murvey Granite Quarry; 53.252134°, −9.510163°).

(Feely, 1982). It is a pink, medium- to coarse-grained granite containing quartz (38%), perthitic orthoclase (33%), plagioclase (albite ~An$_5$) (27%) and biotite (2%) (Figures 8.20a and 8.21a). Pegmatites with quartz and feldspar (green microcline i.e, amazonite) contain clusters (~2 cm across) of cherry red spessartine garnets (Figure 8.20 b), along with spessartine-bearing aplites (Figure 8.21b), are exposed in the CMG quarry (Whitworth and Feely 1989 and 1994). The granite displays both vertical and horizontal joints (Figure 8.20c). The horizontal joints parallel the roof of the intrusion and probably represent cooling joints and/or glacial rebound joints. Dendritic deposits of hematite (iron oxide; Fe$_2$O$_3$), from circulating, iron-rich groundwater, are common on CMGr joints (Figure 8.20d).

REE abundances in the Galway granite is characterised by depletion of light REE and Eu and by enrichment of heavy REE with petrological evolution. The crystal-melt separation of light REE rich accessory phases such as allanite played a key role in the progressive depletion of light REE during magmatic evolution. Eu depletion is linked to the fractionation of feldspar.

FIGURE 8.21
(a) Photomicrograph (XPL) of the Costelloe Murvey Granite. The arrow points to pleochroic halo in the biotite that surrounds U- and Th-bearing accessory minerals, e.g., zircon. (b) Photomicrograph (PPL) of the spessartine-bearing aplite from the Costelloe Murvey Granite Quarry (53.252134°, −9.510163°). Abbreviations: quartz (Qz); biotite (Bt); potassium feldspar (Kfs); plagioclase feldspar (Pl, albite); spessartine (Sps).

The crystallisation of accessories such as xenotime, thorite, uraninite and spessartine garnet is linked to the enrichment of the heavy REE, Y, U and Th in the leucogranite (Murvey Granites) melts and the development of the distinctive gull winged REE profiles in the Costelloe and garnetiferous Roundstone Murvey granite (Feely *et al.*, 1989; Feely *et al.*, 1991).

High radioelement abundances (U ~15 ppm; Th ~40 ppm and K ~4%) make this a High Heat Production (HHP) granite (~7 μWm^{-3}). Its suitability as a Hot Dry Rock (HDR) source of geothermal energy was assessed during the late 1980s and more recently in the 2000s (Feely and Madden, 1986, 1987, 1988; Feely *et al.*, 1989; Feely *et al.*, 1991; Hennessey and Feely 2008 and Farrell *et al.*, 2014, 2015). A vertical, continuously cored borehole (depth: 137.8 m) was drilled into the CMGr in 1982 to determine temperature and heat flow measurements. A thermal gradient of 21.3°C km^{-1}, with a heat flow of 77 mWm^{-2} was determined from this single borehole indicating that the CMGr could be considered as a very low-grade heat source.

Geochronometry of the Galway-Kilkieran Pluton

The geochronology of the granites that comprise the Galway-Kilkieran Pluton reveals emplacement ages for all granites at ~400 Ma which is ~10 million years younger than the Carna Pluton Tables 8.1 and 8.3. However, the CMGr yields an age of ~380 Ma which makes it the youngest of all granites recorded to date in the whole of the Galway Granite Complex (Feely *et al.*, 2010).

Emplacement of the Galway-Kilkieran Pluton

Sinistral movement on the Skird Rocks Fault (SRF) created space for both the magma and stoping of the country rock leading to the formation of the GKP (Leake, 2006). Magma intrusions into the centre of the pluton causing inflation that compressed the peripheral granite and developed a foliation in the Marginal Porphyritic Granodiorite, the Mafic Megacrystic Granodiorite and the Mingling Mixing Zone Granodiorite. A schematic showing the proposed structural control of the emplacement of the GKP adapted from Leake (2006) is presented in Figure 8.22 a, b and c.

Stoped blocks of MMZGr for example, occur in the Knock and Costelloe Murvey Granites while stoped blocks of the MMGr occur in the Shannapheasteen Granodiorite. The deeper level Central Block, uplifted by the Barna and Shannawona Faults, is in faulted contact with the roof zone granites

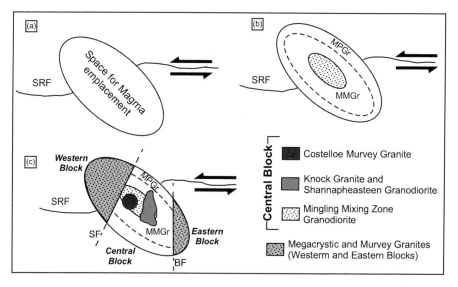

FIGURE 8.22

An emplacement model for the G-KP adapted from Leake (2006). (a) Space is created for magma emplacement by sinistral movement on the SRF; (b) crystallisation starts at the cooler edges of the pluton however, fractionated magmas continue to intrude into the central sector of the pluton causing inflation (ballooning)-related magmatic to submagmatic fabrics in the MPGr, MMGr and the MMZGr (Baxter *et al.*, 2005). (c) The present exposure of the G-KP with the later intrusions, i.e., Shannapheasteen Granodiorite, Knock Granite and the ~380 Ma Costelloe Murvey Granite, that cut the foliated granodiorites, e.g., MMZGr and MMGr. Abbreviations: MPGr: Marginal Porphyritic Granodiorite, MMGr: Mafic Megacrystic Granodiorite, MMZGr: Mingling Mixing Zone Granodiorite, MGr: Megacrystic Granite, SF: Shannawona Fault, BF: Barna Fault and SRF: Skird Rocks Fault.

(i.e., Megacrystic Granite and Murvey Granite) exposed in the Western and Eastern Blocks of the GKP.

In the central sector of the GKP, a major 35° eastward dipping thrust zone, 2 km to the west of the Shannawona Fault Zone (The Furnace Thrust; see Figure 5 in Leake, 2012), has thrust up the deeper crystallised Central Block's MMGr over the Western Block's Megacrystic Granite (MGR). Al-in-hornblende geobarometry of the footwall granite (MGr) and hanging wall granite (MMGr) confirm the thrusting (Callaghan, 2005 and Leake, 2012). According to Leake (2012), the uplift in the Central Block was the result of thrusts and later faults, connected in a complex way, to the intrusive pressures of the later Central Block granites, e.g., the Shannapheasteen, Knock and Costelloe Murvey Granites (Figures 8.13 and 8.22c). Thus, marked westward thrusting that occurs in the GKP in the Camus district attests to a period of strong E-W contraction that contrasts with the late magmatic E-W extension associated with the emplacement of the N-S aplites and late porphyry dikes in the GGC.

Diking in the Galway Granite Complex

Numerous felsitic dikes occur throughout the GGC and its countryrocks (Leake and Tanner, 1994). Two dike suites have been recorded in the Galway Granite Batholith: an early dacite suite derived from the granite magmas and a later mid-Palaeozoic composite dolerite-rhyolite dike suite that represents the final magmatic episode, in the Galway Granite Complex (see Mohr, 2003 and 2004; Feely *et al.*, 2006; Mohr *et al.*, 2018 for details).

References

Baxter, S. 2000. The Geology of Part of the Galway Granite Near Barna, Co. Galway, Ireland. *PhD thesis, National University of Ireland, Galway.*

Baxter, S. and Feely, M. 2002. Magma Mixing and Mingling Textures in Granitoids: Examples from the Galway Granite, Connemara, Ireland. *Mineralogy and Petrology*, 76, 63–7.

Baxter, S., Graham, N.T., Feely, M., Reavy, R.J. and Dewey, J.F. 2005. Fabric Studies of the Galway Granite, Connemara, Ireland. *Geological Magazine*, 142, 81–95.

Callaghan, B. 2005. Locating the Shannwona Fault: Field and Barometric Studies from the Galway Batholith, Western Ireland. *Irish Journal of Earth Sciences*, 23, 85–100.

Coats, J.S. and Wilson, J.R. 1971. The Eastern End of the Galway Granite. *Mineralogical Magazine*, 38, 138–51.

Cobbing, E.J. 1969. The Geology of the District North-West of Clifden, Co Galway. *Proceedings of the Royal Irish Academy*, 67B, 303–25.

Crowley, Q. and Feely, M. 1997. New Perspectives on the Order and Style of Granite Emplacement in the Galway Batholith, Western Ireland. *Geological Magazine*, 134, 539–48.

El Desouky, M., Feely, M. and Mohr, P. 1996. Diorite-Granite Magma Mingling and Mixing Along the Axis of the Galway Granite Batholith, Ireland. *Journal of the Geological Society of London*, 153, 361–74.

Farrell, T., Jones, A., Muller, M., Feely, M., Brock, A., Long, M. and Waters, T. 2014. IRETHERM: The Geothermal Energy Potential of Irish Radiothermal Granites. *EGU General Assembly 2014*, Austria, vol. 16, EGU 2014-6749. 16.

Farrell, T., Muller, M., Rath, V., Feely, M., Jones, A., Brock, A. and The Iretherm Team. 2015. IRETHERM: The Geothermal Energy Potential of Radiothermal Granites in a Low-Enthalpy Setting in Ireland from Magnetotelluric Data. *Proceed World Geothermal Congress 2015*, Melbourne, Australia. 1–10.

Feely, M. 1982. Geological, Geochemical and Geophysical Studies on the Galway Granite in the Costelloe-Inveran Sector, Western Ireland. *PhD thesis, National University of Ireland.*

Feely, M., Coleman, D., Baxter, S. and Miller, B. 2003. U-Pb Zircon Geochronology of the Galway Granite, Connemara, Ireland: Implications for the Timing of Late Caledonian Tectonic and Magmatic Events and for Correlations with Acadian Plutonism in New England. *Atlantic Geology*, 39, 175–84.

Feely, M. and Costanzo, A. 2014. *Galway City Walks: Buildings in Stone.* Galway Civic Trust. 50p. ISBN 978-1-908358-24-0.

Feely, M., Costanzo, A., Gaynor, S.P., Selby, D. and McNulty, E. 2020. A Review of Molybdenite, and Fluorite Mineralisation in Caledonian Granite Basement, Western Ireland, Incorporating New Field and Fluid Inclusion Studies, and Re-Os and U-Pb Geochronology. *Lithos*, 354–355, 1–12.

Feely, M., Gaynor, S., Venugopal, N., Hunt, J. and Coleman, D.S. 2018. New U-Pb Zircon Ages for the Inish Granite Pluton, Galway Granite Complex, Connemara, Western Ireland. *Irish Journal of Earth Sciences*, 36(1), 1–7.

Feely, M., Hunt, J., Lidwill, J. and Barton, K. 2002. *Galway in Stone: A Geological Walk in the Heart of Galway.* Geoscapes. 48p. ISBN 0-9543412-0-1.

Feely, M., Leake, B. E., Baxter, S., Hunt, J. and Mohr, P. 2006. *A Geological Guide to the Granites of the Galway Batholith, Connemara, Western Ireland.* Geological Survey of Ireland, Field Guides Series. 70p. ISBN 1-899702-56-3.

Feely, M. and Madden, J. 1986. A Quantitative Regional Gamma-Ray Survey on the Main Galway Granite, Western Ireland. In: C.J. Andrew, R.W.A. Crowe, S. Finlay, W.M. Pennell and J.F. Pyne (eds.) *Geology and Genesis of Mineral Deposits in Ireland*. Irish Association for Economic Geology. The Irish Association for Economic Geology, c/o Geological Survey of Ireland, Dublin, 195–99.

Feely, M. and Madden, J. 1987. The Spatial Distribution of K, U, Th and Surface Heat Production in the Galway Granite, Connemara, Western Ireland. *Irish Journal of Earth Sciences*, 8, 155–64.

Feely, M. and Madden, J. 1988. Trace Element Variation in the Leucogranites Within the Main Galway Granite, Connemara, Ireland. *Mineralogical Magazine*, 52, 139–46.

Feely, M., McCabe, E. and Kunzendorf, H. 1991. The Evolution of REE Profiles in the Galway Granite, Western Ireland. *Irish Journal of Earth Sciences*, 11, 71–89.

Feely, M., McCabe, E. and Williams, C.T. 1989. U, Th and REE Bearing Accessory Minerals in a High Heat Production (HHP) Leucogranite Within the Galway Granite, Western Ireland. *Transactions of the Institute of Mining and Metallurgy*, 98, B27–B32.

Feely, M., McCarthy, W., Costanzo, A., Leake, B. E. and Yardley, B.W.D. 2022. The Late Silurian to Upper Devonian Galway Granite Complex. In: P.D. Ryan (ed.) *A Field Guide to the Geology of Western Ireland*. Springer Geology Field Guides. Springer Nature, Switzerland, 303–62. Print ISBN 978-3-030-97478-7

Feely, M., Selby, D., Conliffe, J. and Judge, M. 2007. Re-Os geochronology and fluid inclusion microthermometry of molybdenite mineralisation in the late-Caledonian Omey Granite, western Ireland. *Applied Earth Science: Transactions of the Institution of Mining and Metallurgy: Section B* 116(3), 143–49.

Feely, M., Selby, D., Hunt, J. and Conliffe, J. 2010. Long-lived granite-related molybdenite mineralization at Connemara, western Irish Caledonides. *Geological Magazine* 147(6), 886–94.

Ferguson, C.C. and Al-Ameen, S.I. 1985. Muscovite breakdown and corundum growth at anomalously low f H2O: a study of contact metamorphism and convective fluid movement around the Omey granite, Connemara, western Ireland. *Mineralogical Magazine*, 49, 505–15.

Ferguson, C.C. and Harvey, P.K. 1979. Thermally overprinted Dalradian rocks near Cleggan, Connemara, western Ireland. *Proceedings of the Geologists' Association London*, 90, 43–50.

Friedrich, A.M. and Hodges, K.V. 2016. Geological Significance of $^{40}Ar/^{39}Ar$ Mica Dates Across a Mid-Crustal Continental Plate Margin, Connemara (Grampian Orogeny, Irish Caledonides), and Implications for the Evolution of Lithospheric Collisions. *Canadian Journal of Earth Sciences*, 53, 1258–78.

Hennessey, R.W. and Feely, M. 2008. Visualization of Magmatic Emplacement Sequences and Radioelement Distribution Patterns in a Granite Batholith: An Innovative approach using Google Earth. *Journal of the Virtual Explorer*, 29, paper No. 100, 1–14.

Leake, B.E. 1968. Zoned Garnets from the Galway Granite and Its Aplites. *Earth and Planetary Science Letters*, 3, 311–16.

Leake, B.E. 1974. The Crystallization History and Mechanism of Emplacement of the Western Part of the Galway Granite, Connemara, Western Ireland. *Mineralogical Magazine*, 39, 498–13.

Leake, B.E. 1986. The Geology of SW Connemara, Ireland: A Fold and Thrust Dalradian Metagabbroic-Gneiss Complex. *Journal of the Geological Society of London*, 143, 221–36.

Leake, B.E. 2006. Mechanism of Emplacement and Crystallization History of the Northern Margin and Centre of the Galway Granite, Western Ireland. *Transactions of the Royal Society of Edinburgh: Earth Sciences*, 97, 1–23.

Leake, B.E. 2011. Stoping and the Mechanisms of Emplacement of the Granites in the Western Ring Complex of the Galway Granite Batholith, Western Ireland. *Earth and Environmental Science Transactions of the Royal Society of Edinburgh*, 102, 1–16.

Leake, B.E. 2012. Major Thrusting in the Granite and the Role of Late Intrusions in Exposing the Deeper Parts of the Central Block of the Galway Granite Batholith. *Irish Journal of Earth Sciences*, 30, 1–12.

Leake, B.E. and Tanner, P.W.G. 1994. *The Geology of the Dalradian and Associated Rocks of Connemara, Western Ireland*. Royal Irish Academy. 96p. ISBN 1-874045-18-6.

Leake, B.E., Tanner, P.W.G. and Senior, A. 1981 *The Geology of Connemara: Geological Map (1: 63,360) with Cross-Sections, Fold Traces and Metamorphic Isograd Map*. Glasgow University.

Lees, A. and Feely, M. 2016. The Connemara Eastern Boundary Fault: A Review and Assessment Using New Evidence. *Irish Journal of Earth Sciences*, 34, 1–25.

Lees, A. and Feely M. 2017. The Connemara Eastern Boundary Fault: A Correction. *Irish Journal of Earth Sciences*, 35, 55–6.

Max, M.D., Long, C.B. and Geoghegan, M. 1978. The Galway Granite and Its Setting. *Geological Survey of Ireland Bulletin*, 2, 223–33.

McCarthy, W. 2013. An Evaluation of Orogenic Kinematic Evolution Utilizing Crystalline and Magnetic Anisotropy in Granitoids. *PhD thesis, University College Cork, National University of Ireland*.

McCarthy, W., Petronis, M.S., Reavy, R.J. and Stevenson, C.T. 2015a. Distinguishing Diapirs from Inflated Plutons: An Integrated Rock Magnetic Fabric and Structural Study on the Roundstone Pluton, Western Ireland. *Journal of the Geological Society of London*, 172, 550–65.

McCarthy, W., Reavy, R.J., Stevenson, C.T. and Petronis, S. 2015b. Late Caledonian Transpression and the Structural Controls on Pluton Construction; New Insights from the Omey Pluton, Western Ireland. *Earth and Environmental Science Transactions of the Royal Society of Edinburgh*, 106(1), 11–28.

Mohr, P. 2003. Late Magmatism of the Galway Granite Batholith: 1. Dacite Dikes. *Irish Journal of Earth Sciences*, 21, 71–104.

Mohr, P. 2004. Late Magmatism of the Galway Granite Batholith: 11. Composite Dolerite-Rhyolite Dikes. *Irish Journal of Earth Sciences*, 22, 15–32.

Mohr, P., Hunt, J., Riekstins, H. and Kennan, P.S. 2018. Distinguishing Dolerite Dike Populations in Post-Grampian Connemara. *Irish Journal of Earth Sciences*, 36, 1–16.

Murray, J.W. 2009. Wind Transport of Foraminiferal Tests into Subaerial Dunes: An Example from Western Ireland. *Journal of Micropalaeontology*, 28, 185–87.

Pidgeon, S.J. 1969. Zircon U-Pb Ages from the Galway Granite and the Dalradian, Connemara, Ireland. *Scottish Journal of Geology*, 5, 375–92.

Ryan P.D. and Dewey, J.F. 2022. The South Connemara Group. In: P.D. Ryan (ed.) *A Field Guide to the Geology of Western Ireland*. Springer Geology Field Guides. 229–44. Print ISBN 978-3-030-97478-7

Ryan P.D. and Feely, M. 1983. The Main Galway Granite. In: J.B. Archer and P.D. Ryan (eds.) *Geological Guide to the Caledonides of Western Ireland*. Geological Survey of Ireland, Guide Series No. 4. Geological Survey of Ireland, Dublin, 15–18.

Selby, D., Creaser, R.A. and Feely, M. 2004. Accurate Re-Os Molybdenite Dates from the Galway Granite, Ireland. A Critical Comment to: Disturbance of the Re-Os Chronometer of Molybdenites from the Late-Caledonian Galway Granite, Ireland, by Hydrothermal Fluid Circulation. *Geochemical Journal* 38, 291–94.

Streckeisen, A. 1976. To Each Plutonic Rock Its Proper Name. *Earth-Science Reviews*, 12, 1–33.

Townend, R. 1966. The Geology of Some Granite Plutons from Western Connemara, Co. Galway. *Proceedings of the Royal Irish Academy*, 65B, 157–202.

Whitworth, M. and Feely, M. 1989. The Geochemistry of Selected Pegmatites and Their Host Granites from the Galway Granite, Connemara, Ireland. *Irish Journal of Earth Sciences*, 10, 89–97.

Whitworth, M. and Feely, M. 1994. The Compositional Range of Magmatic Mn-Garnets in the Galway Granite, Connemara, Ireland. *Mineralogical Magazine*, 58, 163–68.

Wright, P.C. 1964. The Petrology, Chemistry and Structure of the Galway Granite of the Carna Area, Co. Galway. *Proceedings of the Royal Irish Academy*, 63B, 239–64.

9

Magmatic and Hydrothermal Mineral Deposits in the Galway Granite Complex

Disseminated and quartz vein-hosted Mo-Cu mineralisation occurs through-out the Galway Granite Complex. The most notable occurrences are at the western end of the Galway Granite Batholith: at Mace Head and Murvey in the Carna Pluton. Mo-Cu-bearing quartz veins (~ 5–30 cm thick) trend NE-SW, their orientation controlled by early jointing in the host gran-ite. Additional vein minerals include pyrite, magnetite and muscovite. Mineralised and altered granite extends over an area of at least 2 km^2 and in addition to the vein mineralisation, orbicular granite, quartz-magnetite pods and an intrusive potassium-feldspar breccia also occur. The coastal traverse SW of Mace Pier provides good exposures of disseminated and quartz vein hosted molybdenite, chalcopyrite and pyrite mineralisation. The GGC and the CMC host numerous fluorite veins that also contain a combination of other minerals that include chalcopyrite, galena, pyrite, sphalerite, quartz, calcite, baryte and chlorite. These fluorite veins may be part of the N. Atlantic-European Triassic-Jurassic hydrothermal minerali-sation province.

Introduction

Granite-related Mo-Cu mineralisation and later hydrothermal veins that host a variety of minerals that include fluorite, galena, sphalerite, chalco-pyrite, pyrite, calcite, baryte and quartz occur throughout the GGC. A map detailing the occurrences of the Mo-Cu mineralisation and the later hydro-thermal veins, along with field descriptions, is presented by O'Raghallaigh *et al.* (1997). Selected Mo-Cu mineralisation and fluorite polymineralic vein deposits are highlighted in Figure 9.1.

DOI: 10.1201/9781032698410-9

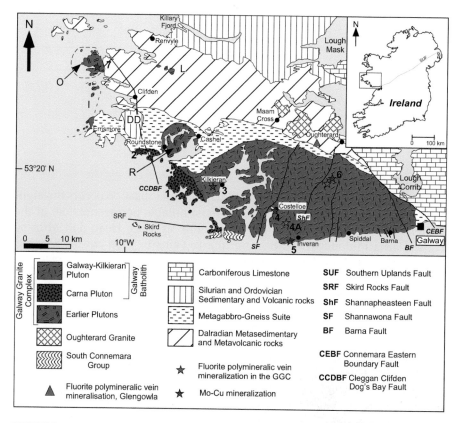

FIGURE 9.1

The geological setting of the Galway Granite Complex and its environs. Mo-Cu mineralisation sites (1: Mace Head; 2: Murvey; 3: Kilkieran; 4: Costelloe road-cutting; 5: Inverin; 6: Larkin's Granite Quarry and 7: Omey Granite), and fluorite polymineralic veins in the GGC (4A: Costelloe Murvey Granite Quarry and 6: Larkin's Granite Quarry) and the CMC (yellow triangle: Glengowla) are highlighted. The Earlier Plutons, Omey (O), Inish (I), Roundstone (R) and Letterfrack (L), are shown. The later Galway Batholith comprises the Carna and Galway-Kilkieran Plutons. The Lower Ordovician Delaney Dome is indicated by the letters DD.

(Map adapted from Townend (1966), Max *et al.* (1978), Leake and Tanner (1994), Pracht *et al.* (2004), Leake (2006), Leake (2011) and Lees and Feely (2016, 2017).)

The Molybdenite-Chalcopyrite (Mo-Cu) Mineralisation

Disseminated and quartz vein-hosted Mo-Cu mineralisation occurs throughout the Galway Granite Complex (Max and Talbot 1986; Derham, 1986; Derham and Feely, 1988; Feely and Hoegelsberger, 1991; Gallagher *et al.*, 1992; Derham, 1993; O'Reilly *et al.*, 1997; Feely *et al.*, 2006; Feely *et al.*, 2007;

Feely *et al.*, 2010 and Feely *et al.*, 2020) (Figure 9.1). The most notable occurrences are at the western end of the Galway Granite Batholith: at Mace Head and Murvey in the Carna Pluton (Loc. 1 and 2 in Figure 9.1). Mo-Cu-bearing quartz veins (~ 5–30 cm thick) trend NE-SW, their orientation controlled by early jointing in the host granite (Derham, 1986; Max and Talbot 1986; McCaffrey *et al.*, 1993). Additional vein minerals include pyrite, magnetite and muscovite. Mineralised and altered granite extends over an area of at least 2 km² and in addition to the vein mineralisation, quartz-magnetite pods (Figure 9.3) and an intrusive potassium-feldspar breccia (Derham and Feely, 1988; Figure 9.2) also occur. The coastal traverse SW of Mace Pier provides good exposures of disseminated and quartz vein hosted molybdenite, chalcopyrite and pyrite mineralisation (Figure 9.2 and Figure 9.3); see Feely *et al.* (2022) for detailed field descriptions and maps.

The Mace Head area was the target for molybdenite exploration by a number of mineral exploration companies, e.g., Anglo United and Canadian Johns Manville during the latter half of the 20th century. More recently, a diamond drilling program (2015) by MOAG Copper Gold Resources Inc. discovered a Mo-Cu mineralised zone of ~1400 x 300 m with mineralisation extending to

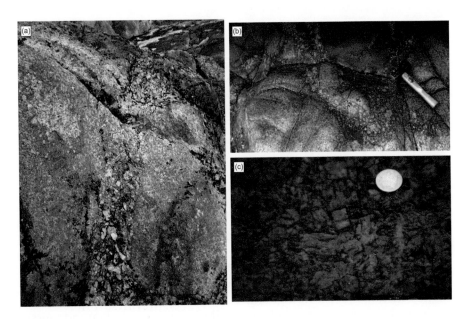

FIGURE 9.2
The Mace Head potassium-feldspar breccia: (a) near vertical breccia vein transecting the Mace Ards Granite; (b) breccia exposure showing angular blocks of host granite and dark grey microdiorite and potassium-feldspar clasts and (c) potassium-feldspar clasts. (Loc 1, Figure 9.1, 53.319721°, −9.898628°).

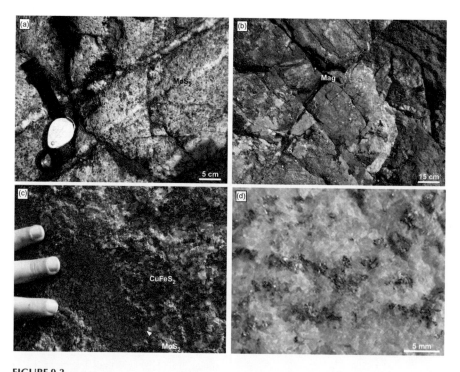

FIGURE 9.3
(a) Quartz vein hosted Mo-Cu mineralisation at Mace Head (Loc 1, Figure 9.1, 53.319721°, −9.898628°). The Mo-Cu is preferentially deposited along the vein walls and disseminations occur within the host Mace-Ards granite. (b) Quartz-Magnetite pods at Mace Head. (Loc 1, Figure 9.1, 53.319721°, −9.898628°). (c) Mo-Cu mineralisation on joint surface at the Costelloe roadside cutting (Loc 4, Figure 9.1, 53.286552°, −9.545798°) and (d) Quartz vein hosted Mo-Cu mineralisation cutting the leucocratic Murvey granite at Kilkieran (Loc 3, Figure 9.1, 53.327603°, −9.748208°).

depths of 200 m. It is controlled by SSW-NNE striking faults in which arrays of Mo-Cu-bearing quartz veins occur. The deposit is cut by later NNW-SSE faults. Diamond drill holes intersected mineralised intervals (~100 m) averaging 0.04% to 0.07% Mo with similar grades for Cu. Locally values of up to 0.36% Mo and 0.32% Cu were reported from drill core.

Intensely altered Murvey leucogranite, (Loc. 2, Figure 9.1), hosts disseminated, and quartz vein hosted Mo-Cu mineralisation intergrown with muscovite. Alteration of the host granite is like that encountered at Mace Head. Feldspars have undergone wholesale kaolinisation, sericitisation and saussuritisation. Muscovite and pyrite replace feldspar and biotite (Gallagher *et al.*, 1992). In 1913 approximately one tonne (=1000 kg) of molybdenum ore of unknown grade was extracted from the Murvey area. The Murvey deposit, however, has been estimated to contain 0.25 million tonnes of molybdenum ore grading at 0.125% Mo (O'Brien, 1959; O'Raghallaigh *et al.*, 1997).

The Mo-Cu Mineralising Fluids: Insights from Fluid Inclusion Studies

Fluid inclusion microthermometry combined with stable isotope studies (O, H, S, C) were used to investigate the genesis of the Mo-Cu mineralisation (Feely and Hoegelsberger, 1991; Gallagher *et al.*, 1992; O'Reilly *et al.*, 1997) in the Galway Granite Complex. These studies, however, were based on the fundamental assumption that the whole of the GGC was ~400 Ma in age and therefore the Mo-Cu mineralisation was also ~400 Ma in age. Leake and Tanner (1994) observed that the whole suite of plutons making up the GGC were late Caledonian and approximately 400 Ma. However, recent geochronology studies, using the U-Pb zircon and Re-Os molybdenite chronometers, have shown that the assembly of the GGC involved five main magmatic episodes extending from *c*.423 Ma to *c*.380 Ma (Buchwaldt *et al.*, 2001; Feely *et al.*, 2003; Selby *et al.*, 2004; Feely *et al.*, 2007; Feely *et al.*, 2010; Feely *et al.*, 2018 and Feely *et al.*, 2020). The earliest magmatic episode *c*.423 Ma was marked by the emplacement of the Omey, Inish and Roundstone Plutons. These were followed by the Carna Pluton (*c*. 410 Ma), the Galway-Kilkieran Pluton (*c*. 400 Ma), then later intrusions at *c*. 380 Ma, e.g., Costelloe Murvey granite (Feely *et al.*, 2010) (Figure 9.1). Finally, the mid-Palaeozoic composite dolerite-rhyolite diking represents the last magmatic episode (Mohr, 2003 and 2004; Mohr *et al.*, 2018). Feely *et al.* (2010) have shown that the temporal assembly of the GGC reflects long-lived granite emplacement (~40 Ma) in tandem with granite-related Mo-Cu mineralisation. The spatial and temporal distribution of the quartz vein hosted Mo-Cu mineralisation and the associated aqueous carbonic mineralising fluids are depicted in Figure 9.4.

Three fluid types (Types 1, 2 and 3) have been identified in granite and vein quartz from across the GGC. Type 1 represents the high-T and moderate salinity aqueous–carbonic fluid responsible for the Mo-Cu mineralisation (Figure 9.5).

Type 2 are magmatic-meteoric aqueous fluids of lower–T and low to moderate salinity (<10 Eq. wt.% NaCl) and occur in granite and vein quartz throughout the GGC and reflect the mixing between magmatic fluids and circulating meteoric fluids during granite emplacement. Type 3 are fluids trapped in the later fluorite (± galena, chalcopyrite, pyrite, sphalerite, baryte, calcite and quartz) veins (see section below). They are $CaCl_2$ -bearing, are more saline (8–28 Eq. wt.% NaCl) and have a lower homogenisation temperature than the earlier fluids (Figure 9.6).

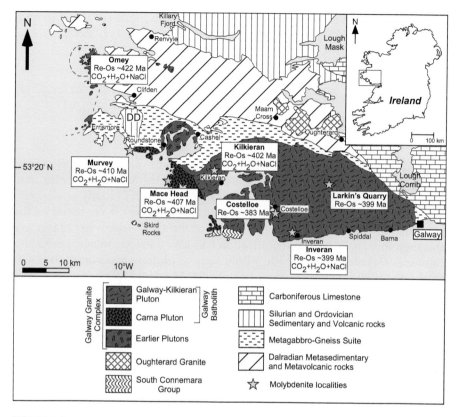

FIGURE 9.4

A simplified geologic map of the Galway Granite Complex (GGC) showing the spatial distribution and temporal range of the Mo-Cu mineralisation, i.e., from ~422 Ma to ~380 Ma. The aqueous-carbonic fluids have been recorded from most of the Mo-Cu-bearing quartz veins across the GGC.

(Data from O'Reilly *et al.* (1997), Feely *et al.* (2010, 2020). Abbreviations: OG: Oughterard Granite; CMC: Connemara Metamorphic Complex; Ord. and Sil.: Ordovician and Silurian rocks; DD: Delaney Dome.)

The Late Fluorite Polymineralic Veins in the GGC

The GGC hosts numerous fluorite veins that contain a combination of other minerals that include chalcopyrite, galena, pyrite, sphalerite, quartz, calcite, baryte and chlorite – see O'Raghallaigh *et al.* (1997) and Moreton and Lawson (2019) for field descriptions of the veins. A selection of these GGC hosted veins is presented in Figure 9.7 and 9.8. Included here are notable examples (Figures 9.7d, 9.8) from the spectacular fluorite vein discovery at Larkin's Granite Quarry (Parkes, 2017, Costanzo and Feely, 2019; Feely *et al.*, 2020;

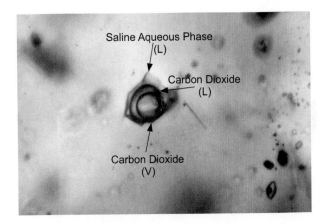

FIGURE 9.5
Photomicrograph of a double bubble fluid inclusion (15 microns, longest dimension) containing the aqueous-carbonic fluid responsible for the Mo-Cu mineralisation in the GGC. The image shows the three-phase inclusion containing two liquid phases (a saline aqueous liquid and carbon dioxide liquid) and a vapour phase (V, carbon dioxide). Section from a Mo-Cu-bearing quartz vein, Mace Head, Carna Pluton. The Mo-Cu mineralisation at Mace Head yields a Re-Os age of 407 Ma (Feely *et al.*, 2010).

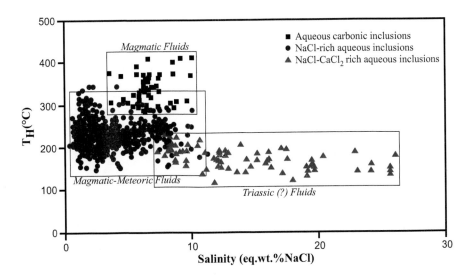

FIGURE 9.6
A bivariate plot of homogenisation temperature (T_H°C) and salinity (Equivalent wt. % NaCl). The three main fluid types recorded in granite quartz and vein minerals (e.g., quartz, fluorite) across the GGC define three fluid composition fields: Magmatic Fluids responsible for the Mo-Cu mineralisation; Magmatic-Meteoric Fluids and Late Fluids associated with fluorite ± base metal, calcite, baryte, chlorite and quartz veins that may be Triassic in age.

FIGURE 9.7

(a) A vein of polychromatic fluorite hosted by intensely altered (chloritised biotite and whole-sale sericitisation of feldspars) Costelloe Murvey Granite. Costelloe Murvey Granite quarry (53.252134°, −9.510163°). (b) Fluorite (Fl)vein with galena (Gn), baryte (Brt), calcite (Cal) and quartz hosted by the Murvey Granite in the Galway-Kilkieran Pluton, Gorumna Island (53.244854°, −9.709153°). (c) Fluorite and sphalerite (Sp)-bearing quartz vein and (d) vuggy vein fluorite aggregate. Both c) and d) are hosted by the Mafic Megacrystic Granite in the Galway-Kilkieran Pluton (Larkin's Granite Quarry; 53.337136°, −9.447362°).

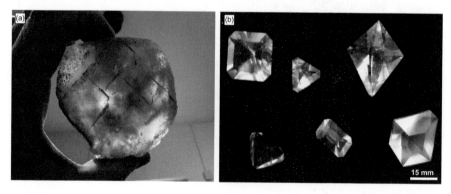

FIGURE 9.8

(a) Backlit single crystal of polychromatic fluorite from Larkin's Granite quarry in the G-KP. (b) A collection of cut fluorite gemstones from Larkin's quarry (53.337136°, −9.447362°). The gemstones were faceted by Mr Simon Zalatel, Geofluids Laboratory, University of Galway.

Sweeney and Unitt, 2021). Sweeney and Unitt (2021) present a comprehensive and illustrated guide to the spectacular fluorite and other vein minerals (e.g., sphalerite and galena) exposed in Larkin's quarry stating that

> Notable mineral occurrences are rare in Ireland, but one exception is the recently discovered fluorite locality of Larkin's quarry in County Galway, which continues to produce a wide variety of aesthetically pleasing fluorite specimens displaying multiple crystal forms and colour zonations.

O'Connor *et al.* (1993) reported that vein fluorite not only postdates the granites of the GGC, but also cuts a late dolerite dike in the Costelloe Murvey Granite Quarry (Loc. 4a in Figure 9.1). Fluid inclusion studies of the vein fluorite, fluorite hosted rare earth element (REE) modelling and $^{40Ar-39}$Ar geochronometry of the dolerite dike indicates that the dolerite dike emplacement and the fluorite mineralisation occurred during the Triassic due to continental rifting of the Atlantic margin in western Ireland. However, Jenkin *et al.* (1997), Menuge *et al.* (1997), O'Reilly *et al.* (1997) and Jenkin *et al.* (1998) all concluded that the Triassic age determined for the dolerite dike (O'Connor *et al.*, 1993) may reflect the timing of the fluorite vein mineralisation only. Mohr *et al.* (2018) argued that the pervasive hydrothermal alteration of the mid-Palaeozoic (late Devonian) dolerite dikes in the GGC, including that from O'Connor *et al.* (1993) depicted in Figure 9.9, reflects the timing of fluorite mineralisation and not dike emplacement. Noteworthy here also are the observations of Leake (1998) regarding the mineralogical evidence for widespread secondary fluid movements throughout the Galway Batholith, the Earlier Plutons and in the country rocks. Leake (1998) described the occurrence of secondary andradite-grossular-hydrogrossular garnet, epidote, prehnite and titanite throughout the GGC and even in some of the country rocks several kilometres from the granites.

Furthermore, O'Reilly *et al.* (1997) argued that the fluorite veins in the GGC are part of the N Atlantic-European Triassic-Jurassic hydrothermal mineralisation province indentified by Mitchell and Halliday (1976). Rifting of the N. Atlantic triggered crustal thinning and subsidence initiating hydrothermal activity at the margins of Mesozoic basins (Mitchell and Halliday, 1976; Halliday and Mitchell, 1984). Jenkin *et al.* (1997) proposed a fluorite vein emplacement model (Figure 9.10) based upon fluid inclusion and stable isotope data that invokes the mixing of moderate salinity Triassic meteoric fluid (Type 1: T = ~205°C and salinity of ~12 Eq. wt.% NaCl) with basinal brines derived from the underlying Carboniferous sequence (Type 2: T = ~125°C and Salinity of >21 Eq. wt.% NaCl). This demonstrates that the GGC was a locus for repeated fluid events; from expulsion of aqueous-carbonic magmatic fluids during the

FIGURE 9.9
The dolerite dike cutting the Costelloe Murvey Granite. Fluorite veins transect this dolerite dike (see Menuge *et al.*, 1997). Costelloe Murvey Granite Quarry (53.252134°, −9.510163°).

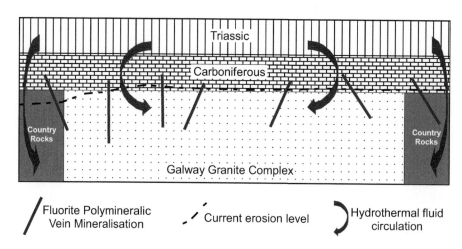

FIGURE 9.10
A schematic E-W cross-section, adapted from Jenkin *et al.* (1997), depicting the formation of the fluorite polymineralic veins due to ingress of Triassic hydrothermal fluids passing through the rocks of the Carboniferous and the Connemara Metamorphic Complex.

spatial and temporal assembly of the complex, through a mixing of magmatic and meteoric fluid convection systems to later (Triassic?) hydrothermal mineralisation.

Late Fluorite Polymineralic Veins in the Connemara Metamorphic Complex

Similar late fluorite polymineralic vein mineralisation occurs within the Connemara Metamorphic Complex. Their spatial distribution along with field descriptions are presented in Reynolds *et al.* (1990). In general, three broad styles of mineralisation in the CMC were described by McArdle *et al.* (1986), i.e., Type 1: stratabound sulphide deposits, Type 2: Oughterard Granite–associated skarn deposits and Type 3: post deformation vein hosted base metal (galena, sphalerite, chalcopyrite, pyrite) and baryte mineralisation. The latter type also contain fluorite, calcite and quartz and are possibly temporal equivalents to the veins hosted by GGC.

Kennan *et al.* (1988) noted that these base metal deposits in the Connemara Metamorphic Complex are often fault hosted, unrelated to igneous activity and distinct from the earlier Type1 stratabound sulphide deposits and Type 2 skarn deposits. One outstanding example of this style of mineralisation is the Glengowla East mine, where an east-west trending vuggy lode with fluorite-calcite-barite-quartz-galena-pyrite-chalcopyrite-sphalerite is hosted by the Middle Dalradian Lakes Marble Formation. A selection of vein minerals from Glengowla is presented in Figure 9.11. O'Reilly *et al.* (1997) argued that fluid inclusion and stable isotope studies, of the Glengowla vein deposit, indicate similar fluid signatures involving Carboniferous and Triassic fluid mixing (Figure 9.10) to those associated with the fluorite polymineralic veins in the GGC. Finally, concordant K-Ar dates at 212.4 Ma for Glengowla vein material may reflect the timing of ore formation (Halliday and Mitchell, 1983).

The geology and history of the mine has been described in detail by Moreton (2019). This 19th-century mine is located approximately 3km WSW of Oughterard (Figure 9.1). Four shafts are still evident at the surface, and extant mine buildings include the mine captain's house and the explosives magazine. The mine was active between 1851 and 1852 when 36 tonnes of galena (including 140 oz of silver) were recovered. Records also state that the mine was worked between 1860 and 1865 for galena, sphalerite and barite. It was abandoned and flooded by 1870. The working reached a depth of approximately 32 m and a lateral extent of 108 m. The mine has been rehabilitated and upgraded to a heritage mine (by the Geoghegan family) and is open to the public for most of the year.

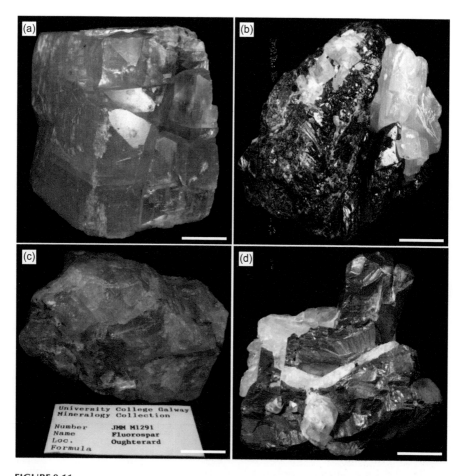

FIGURE 9.11
A selection of vein minerals from Glengowla Mine. (a) calcite, (b) sphalerite, (c) fluorite and (d) galena. These samples form part of the Connemara mineral collection in the James Mitchell Museum, University of Galway (Feely et al., 1996). Scale = 5 cm.

References

Buchwaldt, R., Kroner, A., Toulkeredes, T., Todt, W. and Feely, M. 2001. Geochronology and Nd-Sr Systematics of Late Caledonian Granites in Western Ireland: New Implications for the Caledonian Orogeny. *Geological Society of America Abstracts with Programs*, 33(1), A32.

Costanzo, A. and Feely, M. 2019. A Review of Important Gem Materials from Connemara, Western Ireland. International Gemmological Conference, Nantes, France. *Proceedings of the 36th International Gemmological Conference*. 58–60.

Derham, J.M. 1986. Structural Control of Sulphide Mineralization at Mace Head, Co. Galway. In: C. J. Andrews, R. W. A. Crowe, S. Finlay, W. M. Pennell and J. Pyne (eds.) *Geology and Genesis of Mineral Deposits in Ireland,* Irish Association for Economic Geology, pp. 187–93.

Derham, J.M. 1993. The geology and genesis of the Mace Head molybdenite deposit, Carna, Co. Galway, Ireland, Ph.D. Thesis, National University of Ireland.

Derham, J.M., and Feely, M. 1988. A K-Feldspar Breccia from the Mo-Cu Stockwork Deposit in the Galway Granite, West of Ireland. *Journal of the Geological Society of London,* 145, 661–667.

Feely, M., Coleman, D., Baxter, S. and Miller, B. 2003. U-Pb Zircon Geochronology of the Galway Granite, Connemara, Ireland: Implications for the Timing of late Caledonian Tectonic and Magmatic Events and for Correlations with Acadian Plutonism in New England. *Atlantic Geology,* 39, 175–184.

Feely, M., Costanzo, A., Gaynor, S.P., Selby, D., McNulty, E., 2020. A Review of Molybdenite, and Fluorite Mineralization in Caledonian Granite Basement, Western Ireland, Incorporating New Field and Fluid Inclusion Studies, and Re-Os and U-Pb Geochronology. *Lithos,* 354–355, 1–12.

Feely, M., Gaynor, S., Venugopal, N., Hunt, J. and Coleman, D.S. 2018. New U-Pb Zircon Ages for the Inish Granite Pluton, Galway Granite Complex, Connemara, Western Ireland. *Irish Journal of Earth Sciences,* 36 (1): 1–7.

Feely, M., Harper, D.A.T. and Madden, M. 1996. Displays and Exceptional Collections. In: Harper, D.A.T. (ed.) *An Irish Geological Time Capsule,* published by James Mitchell Museum, University of Galway. ISBN 0 952957108. Standard Printers, Galway, pp. 46–57.

Feely, M. and Hoegelsberger, H. 1991. Preliminary Fluid Inclusion Studies of the Mace Head Mo-Cu Deposit in the Galway Granite. *Irish Journal of Earth Sciences,* 11, 1–10.

Feely, M., Leake, B., Baxter, S., Hunt, J and Mohr, P. 2006. A Geological Guide to the Granites of the Galway Batholith, Connemara, Western Ireland. *Geological Survey of Ireland, Field guides Series.* 70pp. ISBN 1-899702-56-3

Feely, M., McCarthy, W., Costanzo, A., Leake, B.E.L. and Yardley, B.W.D. 2022. The Late Silurian to Upper Devonian Galway Granite Complex. In: P.D. Ryan(ed.) *A Field Guide to the Geology of Western Ireland.* Springer Geology Field Guides. Print ISBN 978-3-030-97478-7; 303–362.

Feely, M., Selby, D., Conliffe, J. and Judge, M. 2007. Re-Os Geochronology and Fluid Inclusion Microthermometry of Molybdenite Mineralisation in the Late-Caledonian Omey Granite, Western Ireland. *Applied Earth Science,* 116(3), 143–149.

Feely, M., Selby, D., Hunt, J. and Conliffe, J. 2010. Long-lived Granite-Related Molybdenite Mineralization at Connemara, Western Irish Caledonides. *Geological Magazine,* 147(6), 886–894.

Gallagher, V., Feely, M., Hoegelsberger, H., Jenkin, G.R.T. and Fallick, A.E. 1992. Geological, Fluid Inclusion and Stable Isotope Studies of Mo Mineralization, Galway Granite, Ireland. *Mineralium Deposita,* 27, 314–325.

Halliday, A.N. and Mitchell, J.G. 1983. K-Ar Ages of Clay Concentrates from Irish Orebodies and Their Bearing on the Timing of Mineralisation. *Earth and Environmental Sc. Trans. Royal Soc. Edinburgh,* V74(1), 1–14.

Halliday, A.N. and Mitchell, J.G. 1984. K-Ar Ages of Clay-Size Concentrates from the Mineralisation of the Pedroches Batholith, Spain, and Evidence for Mesozoic Hydrothermal Activity Associated with the Break-up of Pangaea. *Earth Planetary Science Letters*, 68, 229–239.

Jenkin, G.R.T., Mohr, P., Mitchell, J.G., Fallick, A.E. 1998. Carboniferous Dykes as Monitors of Post-Caledonian Fluid Events in West Connacht, Ireland. *Transactions of the Royal Society of Edinburgh: Earth Sciences*, 89, 225–243.

Jenkin, G.R.T., O'Reilly, C., Feely, M. and Fallick, A.E. 1997. The geometry of mixing of surface and basinal fluids in the Galway Granite, Connemara, Western Ireland. *Proc. Geofluids II, Queens University Belfast*, 97: 374–377.

Kennan, P.S., McArdle, P., Gallagher, V., Morris, J.H., O'Connor, P.J., O'Keefe, W.G., Reynolds, N. and Steed, G.M. 1988. A study of the contribution of isotope geology in the development of exploration strategy. Comm European Communities Rep EUR11628 EN

Leake, B.E. 2006. Mechanism of Emplacement and Crystallisation History of the Northern Margin and Centre of the Galway Granite, Western Ireland. *Transactions of the Royal Society of Edinburgh: Earth Sciences*, 97, 1–23.

Leake, B.E. 2011. Stoping and the Mechanisms of Emplacement of the Granites in the Western Ring Complex of the Galway Granite Batholith, Western Ireland. *Earth and Environmental Science Transactions of the Royal Society of Edinburgh*, 102, 116.

Leake, B.E. 1998. Widespread Secondary Ca Garnet and Other Ca Silicates in the Galway Granite and Its Satellite Plutons Caused by Fluid Movements, Western Ireland. *Mineralogical Magazine*, 62, 381–386.

Leake, B.E., Tanner, P.W.G. 1994. *The Geology of the Dalradian and Associated Rocks of Connemara, Western Ireland*. R Irish Acad Dublin, 96pp.

Lees, A., Feely, M. 2016. The Connemara Eastern Boundary Fault: A Review and Assessment Using New Evidence. *Irish Journal of Earth Sciences*, 34, 1–25.

Lees, A., Feely, M. 2017. The Connemara Eastern Boundary Fault: a correction. *Irish Journal of Earth Sciences* 35: 55–56.

Max, M.D., Long, C.B., Geoghegan, M. 1978. The Galway Granite and its setting. *Geological Survey Ireland Bulletin*, 2, 223–233.

Max, M.D. and Talbot, V. 1986. Molydenum concentrations in the western end of the Galway Granite and their structural setting. In: C. J. Andrews, R. W. A. Crowe, S. Finlay, W. M. Pennell & J. Pyne (eds.) *Geology and Genesis of Mineral Deposits in Ireland*, Irish Association for Economic Geology, 177–185.

McArdle, P., Schaffalitzky, C., Reynolds, N., Bell, A.M. 1986. Controls on Mineralization in the Dalradian of Ireland. In: C. J. Andrews, R. W. A. Crowe, S. Finlay, W. M. Pennell & J. Pyne (eds.) *Geology and Genesis of Mineral Deposits in Ireland*, 31–44. Irish Association for Economic Geology.

McCaffrey, K., Johnson, D., Feely, M. 1993. Use of Fractal Statistics in the Analysis of Mo-Cu Mineralisation at Mace Head, County Galway. *Irish Journal of Earth Sciences*, 12, 139–148.

Menuge, J. F., Feely, M. and O'Reilly, C. 1997. Origin and Granite Alteration Effects of Hydrothermal Fluid: Isotopic Evidence from Fluorite Veins, Co. Galway, Ireland. *Mineralium Deposita*, 32, 34–43.

Mitchell, J.G. and Halliday, A.N. 1976. Extent of Triassic/Jurassic Hydrothermal Ore Deposits on the North Atlantic Margins. *Transactions of the Institution of Mining and Metallurgy*, B85, 159–161.

Mohr, P. 2003. Late Magmatism of the Galway Granite Batholith: 1. Dacite dikes. *Irish Journal of Earth Sciences*, 21, 71–104.

Mohr, P. 2004. Late Magmatism of the Galway Granite Batholith: 11. Composite Dolerite-rhyolite Dikes. *Irish Journal of Earth Sciences*, 22, 15–32.

Mohr, P., Hunt, J., Riekstins, H. and Kennan, P.S. 2018. Distinguishing Dolerite Dike Populations in Post-Grampian Connemara. *Irish Journal of Earth Sciences*, 36, 1–16.

Moreton, S. 2019. Glengowla: From Lead Mine to Show Mine. *Journal of the Mining Heritage Trust of Ireland*, 17, 3–14.

Moreton, S. and Lawson, R. 2019. Fluorite and Associated Minerals from Lettermuckoo Quarry, Connemara, Co. Galway. *Journal of the Russell Society*, 38–42.

O'Brien, M.V. 1959. The future of non-ferrous mining in Irelan. In: *The Future of Non-Ferrous Mining in Great Britain and Ireland*. Institute of Mining & Metallurgy, London, 5–25.

O'Raghallaigh, C., Feely, M., McArdle, P., MacDermot, C., Geoghegan, M., and Keary, R. 1997. Mineral Localities in the Galway Bay Area. Geol Sur Ireland, Report Series RS97/1 (Mineral Resources). 1–63.

O'Connor, P.J., Hogelsberger, H., Feely, M. & Rex, D.C. 1993. Fluid Inclusion Studies, Rare-Earth Element Chemistry and Age of Hydrothermal Fluorite Mineralization in Western Ireland - A Link with Continental Rifting? *Transactions of the Institute of Mining & Metallurgy*, B102, 141–148.

O'Reilly, C., Jenkin, G.R.T., Feely, M., Alderton, D.H.M. and Fallick, A.E. 1997. A Fluid Inclusion and Stable Isotope Study of 200 Ma of Fluid Evolution in the Galway Granite, Connemara, Ireland. *Contributions to Mineralogy & Petrology*, 129, 120–142.

Parkes, M. 2017. Fluorite Find in Connemara. *Earth Science Ireland*, 22, 14.

Pracht, M., Lees, A., Leake, B., Feely, M., Long, B., Morris, J. and McConnell, B. 2004. Geology of Galway Bay: A geological description to accompany the Bedrock Geology 1:100,000 Scale Map Series, Sheet 14, Galway Bay. Geol Sur Ire. pp76.

Reynolds, N., McArdle, P., Pyne, J.F., Farrell, L.P.C. and Flegg, A.M. 1990. *Mineral Localities in the Dalradian and Associated Rocks Igneous Rocks of Connemara, County Galway*. Geol. Surv. Ireland Report Series. 89pp.

Selby, D., Creaser, R.A. and Feely, M. 2004. Accurate Re-Os Molybdenite Dates from the Galway Granite, Ireland. A Critical Comment to: Disturbance of the Re-Os Chronometer of Molybdenites from the Late-Caledonian Galway Granite, Ireland, by Hydrothermal Fluid Circulation. *Geochemical Journal*, 38, 291–294.

Sweeney, M. and Unitt, R. 2021. Larkin's Quarry, Connemara, Ireland. *Mineralogical Record*, 52(2), 129–156.

Townend, R. 1966. The Geology of Some Granite Plutons from Western Connemara, Co. Galway, *Proceedings of the Royal Irish Academy*, 65B, 157–202.

Index

Pages in *italics* refer to figures and pages in **bold** refer to tables.

A

Al-Ameen, S.I., 98, 119
alkali feldspar granite, 95–96
amphibolites, 36, 59, 63
andalusite, 61, *62*, 98, 119
Appin Group, 14–15
   Connemara Marble Formation,
     22–23, *24*
Atherton, M.P., *105*
aureole rocks, of Galway Granite
     Complex, 98, *99*

B

Ballynakill Schist Formation, 29, 64, *64*
Barber, J.P., 67
Barnanoraun Schist Formation, 19–20,
     23, 25, *25*, 64, *66*
Barrovian garnet zone, 63
Barrovian metamorphism, 59–61, **61**,
     62, 63
   medium-pressure, 79, 85
Barrovian zones, 60
Barrow, G., 60
Baxter, S., 136
Ben Levy Grit Formation, 31–32
Bennabeola Quartzite Formation, 26–27,
     28–29, 33, *34*, 122
   D4 antiform by, 45
   quartzites of, 45
Buchan metamorphism, 59–60, **61**, *62*,
     63–64

C

calcite (Cal), 68, *70*
Caledonian Orogeny, 109
Carboniferous limestone, *10*, 92, 134, *135*
Carna Granite (CG), 123–124, *124*

Carna Pluton, 1, 92, 103, 107, 109–110,
     110
   Carna Granite, 123–124, *124*
   Cuilleen Granite, 123
   emplacement of, 95
   Errisbeg Townland Granite, 123–127,
     124, *126*, *128*
   feldspar compositions in, 129
   Gorteen Bay and Dog's Bay, 124, *127*
   granites of, 115
   Mace-Ards granite, 127, *129*
   Metagabbro Gneiss Suite, 123, *126*
   Mo-Cu mineralisation, 128
   Murvey Granite, 127, *128*
   QAP ternary diagram, *125*, 127
Cashel Hill, 6, *7*
Cashel-Lough Wheelaun-
     Loughaunanny intrusion, 36,
     36, 52, *52–53*, 67
Cashel Schist Formation, 31, 37, *38*,
     66–67
Cathedral of Our Lady Assumed into
     Heaven and St Nicholas, 134,
     135
CCDBF, *see* Cleggan-Clifden-Dog's Bay
     Fault
centimetric-scale waxy green crystals, of
     cordierite, 66, *67*
centimetric-to kilometric-scale folds, 41,
     44, *44*, *46*, *50*
central block, granites of, **132**, 135–136
CG, *see* Carna Granite
Claddagh Dominican Church
     (19th-century), 134, *135*
Cleggan Boulder Bed Formation
     Argyll Group, 25, *26*
     cobblestones, 25, *27*
Cleggan-Clifden-Dog's Bay Fault
     (CCDBF), 107, *108–109*, 124, *127*
Clifden Schist Formation, 19–20

164

Cliff, R.A., 71, 78, *86*, 87, 89, 98
Clift, P.D., 78
CMC, *see* Connemara Metamorphic
    Complex
CMGr, *see* Costelloe Murvey Granite
Coats, J.S., 131
Conmaícne Mara, 2
Connemara
    geographical setting and geology,
        1–3, *2–4*
    glacial landscapes of, 8–10, *9–11*
    Metamorphic and Granite Terranes,
        3, *4*
    metamorphic and igneous rocks,
        spatial distribution of, 4, *5*
Connemara Antiform, 15
Connemara Basement, *10*
Connemara Dalradian pelites,
    metamorphism of, 60–61, **61**,
    62–66, *63–64*
Connemara Eastern Boundary Fault,
    107, *108–109*
Connemara Marble Formation, 15
    Appin Group, 22–23, *24*
    folded marble horizons in, 33
    Lissoughter Hill view, *20*
    Lough Derryclare marble exposure,
        21
    marble outcrop of, 21–22, *22*
    metamorphism, 68–71, *69–70*
    polished slabs of, *23*
Connemara Metamorphic Complex
    (CMC), 1–2
    Dalradian metamorphosed
        sedimentary and igneous
        rocks, 4–6
    Dalradian rocks, of northern belt, *see*
        Dalradian lithostratigraphy
    deformation phases, 41, *42–43*, 43
        northern belt, 43–45, *44–51*
        relative timing of, 78–85
        southern belt, 47, *52*, 52–53, *53*
    fluorite polymineralic veins in, 159,
        160
    geology of, *16–17*
    in Grampian terrane, 83–85, *84*
    magmatism, 78–85
    Metagabbro Gneiss Suite, 4, 6–8, *7*

Metamorphic Highlands of, 3, 5
metamorphic rocks, *see*
    metamorphism
previously published ages
    recalculations from, 78
southern belt, *see* Metagabbro Gneiss
    Suite
time-related NW-SE cross-sections,
    78–79, *79–83*, 83
Connemara Synform, 45
contact metamorphism, 98
cordierite, 72, 119
    centimetric-scale waxy green crystals
        of, 66, *67*
Cornamona Marble Formation, 31–32
Costelloe Murvey Granite (CMGr),
    140–143, *141–142*
    emplacement of, 95, 103, 107,
        109–110
Costelloe Murvey Granite Quarry, 157,
    158
County Galway, 1–2, *2*
    spatial distribution, of major glacial
        landforms, *9*, 10
Crag antiform, 45
Crowley, Q., 136, 153
Cuilleen Granite, 123, 129
Cur Hill-Maumeen P-T-t path, 87, 89

D

D2 Derryclare Fold, 41, 44, *46*
    N-S structural profile, 45, *47*
D3 Glencoaghan antiform, 45, *48–49*
D3 Quarry Antiform, 45, *50–51*
D4 Connemara antiform, 41, 45, *46*, 119
    axial trace of, *48–49*
    N-S structural profile, 45, *47*
Dalradian Connemara Marble
    Formation, 59
Dalradian lithostratigraphy, 14, 19, **19**
    Ballynakill Schist Formation, 29
    Barnanoraun Schist Formation, 23,
        25, *25*
    Ben Levy Grit Formation, 32
    Bennabeola Quartzite Formation,
        26–27, *28–29*
    Cashel Schist Formation, 31

Cleggan Boulder Bed Formation, 25, 26–27
Clifden Schist Formation, 19–20
of Connemara Dalradian rocks, 19, **19**
Connemara Marble Formation, 20–23, *20–24*, 31–32
geology and topography correlations, 33, *34*
Grampian Terrane map, *18*, 18–19
Kylemore Schist Formation, 31, *32*
Lakes Marble Formation, 28–29, *30–31*
Lough Kilbride Schist Formation, 32–33
northern belt, 15, *16–17*
Streamstown Schist Formation, 27, *30*
Dalradian metamorphosed sedimentary and igneous rocks, 1, 4–6
Dawros-Currywongaun-Doughruagh Complex (DCDC), 71
Dawros-Currywongaun-Doughruaigh (D-C-D), 8, *16–17*, 32, 35
deformation, relative timing of, 78–85
Delaney Dome (DD), 1, 6, *63*; *see also* Delaney Dome Metarhyolite Formation; Ordovician Delaney Dome
Delaney Dome Metarhyolite Formation, 53–54, *54–55*, 56, 79, *82*
DEM, *see* digital elevation model
Dewey, J.F., 98
diamond drilling program, 151
digital elevation model (DEM), 33
dolomite (Dol), 68, *70*
Downs-Rose, K., 36, 52, 71
Draut, A.E., 78
Drumlin, 9–10

E

Earlier Plutons, 92, 98, 109, *110*
emplacement of, 94–95
Inish Pluton, 119–120, *120*
inter-and intra-granite variations, 115, *116*
Letterfrack Pluton, *122*, 122–123
Omey Pluton, 116–119, *117–118*
QAP ternary diagram, 115, *116*

Roundstone Pluton, 120–122, *121*
eastern block, 133–134, *134–135*
El Desouky, M., 136–137
Errisbeg Townland Granite (ETG), 123–127, *124*, *126*, *128*, 129
Errismore-Roundstone-Gowla intrusion, 35, 67, *68*
ETG, *see* Errisbeg Townland Granite
E-W Mannin Antiform, 41, 56, 87
E-W metamorphic zones, 59, 63, *63*
E-W Steep Belt, 45
E-W striking Scandian folding, 41, 87

F

Feely, M., 33, 67, 96, 119, 136
Ferguson, C.C., 98, 119
fluid inclusion, Mo-Cu mineralisation, 153, *154–155*
fluorite polymineralic veins
in Connemara Metamorphic Complex, 159, *160*
in GGC, 154, *156*, 157, *158*, 159
fluorite vein emplacement model, 157, *158*
Friedrich, A.M., 78, 84–87, *86*, 120

G

Gabbros, 6
Galway Batholith, 123
Carna Pluton, 123–128, *124–129*
Galway-Kilkieran Pluton, *130*, 130–131, *131*, **132**
Galway Granite Complex (GGC), 1–4, 41, *43*, 87, **88**
aureole rocks of, 98, *99*
ballooning and block stoping in, 110–111, *111–112*
Carboniferous limestones, 92
Carna Pluton, 123–128, *124–129*
central block, 135–136
classification of, 95–96
Costelloe Murvey Granite, 140–143, *141–142*
description of, 8
diking in, 145
Earlier Plutons, *see* Earlier Plutons

in eastern block, 133–134, *134–135*
episodic magmatism, 103
fluorite polymineralic veins in, 154, *156*, 157, *158*, 159
Galway-Kilkieran Pluton, *130*, 130–131, *131*, **132**, 143–144
geochemical characteristics of, 96, *97*
geochronology of, *94*, 94–95
geological setting of, 92, *93–94*
Iapetus Ocean closure, 103–104, *104*
Knock Granite, 140
lithologies of, 92
Lough Lurgan Granite, 140
Mafic Megacrystic Granodiorite, 136, *137*
magma generation, 103–105, *104–105*
Marginal Porphyritic Granodiorite, 136
Mingling Mixing Zone Granodiorite, 136–137, *138–139*
Mo-Cu mineralisation, 149–154
petrology and mineralogy of, 95
Shannapheasteen Granodiorite, 140
structural controls on ascent of, *106*, 106–110, *108–110*
western block, 133
Galway-Kilkieran Pluton (G-KP), 1, 92, 103, *106*, 107, 109, *110*, 123
emplacement of, 95, 143–144, *144*
faults, 130
geochronometry of, 131, **132**, 143
geological map of, *130*
granites of, 115
plagioclase feldspar, 131, **132**
potassium-feldspar in, 131
QAP ternary diagram, 131, *131*
geochronology, of Galway Granite Complex, **88**, *94*, 94–95
geochronometry, 78
of Delaney Dome Metarhyolite Formation, 56, 84–85
of Galway-Kilkieran Pluton, 131, **132**
GGC, *see* Galway Granite Complex
Ghani, A.A., *105*
G-KP, *see* Galway-Kilkieran Pluton
Gorteen Bay, 124, *127*
Grampian Orogeny, 5, 25, 75–76, 77, 78
Grampian Terrane, *18*, 18–19, 83–85, *84*

granite magmatism, 35, 103–104, *104*
granulites, of Metagabbro Gneiss Suite, 66–68, *66–68*

H

Halliday, A.N., 157
Harvey, P.K., 98
Hennessy, R., 33
High Heat Production (HHP) granite, 143
Highland Boundary Fault (HBF), 83, *84*, 107
high-T-low-P metamorphism, 85–86, 89
Hodges, K.V., 78, 84–87, *86*, 120
hot oceanic island arc, 79

I

Iapetus Ocean, 75–76, *76–77*
closure of, 103–104, *104*, 106, *106*
index minerals, 60–61
Inish Granite (IG), *63*
Inish Pluton, 98, 119–120, *120*

J

Johnson, E.A., 95
Joyces Antiform, 45

K

Kennan, P.S., 159
KGr, *see* Knock Granite
Killannin-Tullokyne esker, 10
Knock Granite (KGr), 140
Knock-Knockarasser-Gortgar drumlin swarm, *11*
kyanite, 61, *62*
Kylemore Schist Formation, 31, *32*, 64, *65*

L

Lakes Marble Formation, 28–29, *30–31*, 98
Letterfrack Pluton, 122–123
Omey Pluton, 116

pelites and carbonates of, 119
steep belt, 45
Upper Marble Member of, 45, *51*
Lawson, R., 154
Leake, B.E., 19–20, 31–33, 36, 52, 56, 71,
    83, 87, 98, 109, 153, 157
Letterfrack Pluton, 98, 115, *122*, 122–123
leucogranites, 96
LLGr, *see* Lough Lurgan Granite
Lough Kilbride Schist Formation, 32–33
Lough Lurgan Granite (LLGr), 140
Lough Nafooey Island, 76, *77*, 78, *79*
Lough Nahasleam migmatites P-T-t
    path, 89

M

Mace-Ards granite, 127, 129, *129*
Mace Head, Mo-Cu mineralisation at,
    151, 151–152, *152*
Mafic Megacrystic Granodiorite
    (MMGr), 136, *137*
mafic microgranular enclaves (MME),
    136–137
magmatism, 78–85, **88**
Main Inish Granite, 119
Mannin thrust, 1, 8, 75, 83–84
    Delaney Dome and, 53–54, *54–55*, 56
    Metagabbro Gneiss Suite, 79, *82*
    on P-T-t path, 87
marble *sensu stricto*, 69, 71
Marginal Granite, 119
Marginal Porphyritic Granodiorite
    (MPGr), 136
Maumturk Quartzite Mountains, glacial
    valley of, *11*
McArdle, P., 159
McCarthy, W., 107
Megacrystic Granite (MGr)
    in eastern block, 133
    pillar, 134, *135*
    in western block, 133
metabasites, 71
Metagabbro Gneiss Suite (MGGS), 1, 4,
    6–8, *7*, 14, 79, *82*, 111
    arc-related gabbros of, 85
    dark grey bedrock, 133, *134*

gabbros and peridotites of, 79
integral components of, 87
metagabbros, 15, *16–17*, 33, *35*, 35–36,
    36
migmatites and granulites of, 66–68,
    66–68
orthogneisses, 15, *16–17*, 36–37, *37–38*
paragneisses, 15, *16–17*, 36–37, *37–38*
in southern Connemara, 79, *81*
metagabbros, 15, *16–17*, 33, *35*, 35–36,
    36, 52
Metamorphic Grade, **61**
metamorphism, **88**
    of Connemara Dalradian pelites,
        60–61, **61**, *62–66*, 63–64
    Connemara Marble Formation,
        68–71, *69–70*
    in Connemara Metamorphic
        Complex, 78–85
    metabasites, 71
    MGGS, migmatites and granulites of,
        66–68, *66–68*
    overview of, 59–60
    retrograde, 71–72, *72*
metasediments, 52
MGGS, *see* Metagabbro Gneiss Suite
MGr, *see* Megacrystic Granite
Midlandian, 9
migmatites, of Metagabbro Gneiss Suite,
    66–68, *66–68*
mineralogy, of Galway Granite
    Complex, 95
Mingling Mixing Zone Granodiorite
    (MMZGr), 136–137, *138–139*
Mitchell, J.G., 157
MME, *see* mafic microgranular enclaves
MMGr, *see* Mafic Megacrystic
    Granodiorite
MMZGr, *see* Mingling Mixing Zone
    Granodiorite
MOAG Copper Gold Resources Inc., 151
Mo-Cu mineralisation, *see* molybdenite-
    chalcopyrite (Mo-Cu)
    mineralisation
Mohr, P., 157
molybdenite-chalcopyrite (Mo-Cu)
    mineralisation, 128, 149, *150*

disseminated and quartz vein-hosted, 150–151
fluid inclusion microthermometry, 153, *154–155*
Mace Head, *151*, 151–152, *152*
Murvey deposit, 152–153
Moreton, S., 154, 159
MPGr, *see* Marginal Porphyritic Granodiorite
Murvey Granite, 96, 127, *128*, 129
in eastern block, 133–134, *134–135*
in western block, 133

N

NNE-trending Shannawona Fault, 130
northern belt, 15; *see also* Dalradian lithostratigraphy
crossection (A-B), *46*
deformation phases, 43–45, *44–51*
N-S Dolan Antiform, 41, 56, 87
NW-SE cross-sections, time-related, 78–79, *79–83*, 83
NW-trending Barna Fault, 130

O

O'Connor, P.J., 157
Omey Granite (OmG), *63*
Omey Pluton, 116–119, *117–118*
aureole rocks, 98
O'Raghallaigh, C., 149, 154
Ordovician Delaney Dome, 1–2, *7*
Ordovician South Connemara Group, 2–3
O'Reilly, C., 157, 159
orthoclase, 95
orthogneisses, 15, *16–17*, 36–37, *37–38*, 52
Oughterard Granite (OG), 2, *63*, 83, *83*, 87, 89, 98

P

palaeosome, 37
paragneisses, 15, *16–17*, 36–37, *37–38*
pelitic rocks, 59–60

petrology, of Galway Granite Complex, 95
phacolith, 119
pinitised cordierite porphyroblasts, 31, *32*, 98, *99*
plagioclase feldspar granite, 95–96, 129
plane polarised light (PPL), *64*, *65*
plate tectonic model, 56
porphyroblastic garnets and feldspar, internal S1 fabrics in, 41, 43–44
potassium feldspar, 129, 131, **132**, 136
gneisses, 36, *37*
Pressure-Temperature-time (P-T-t) paths, 85
Cliff, R.A.
Cur Hill-Maumeen, 87, 89
Lough Nahasleam migmatites, 89
Friedrich, A.M., 85–87, *86*, **88**
Hodges, K.V., 85–87, *86*, **88**
Yardley, B.W.D.
Cur Hill-Maumeen, 87, 89
Lough Nahasleam migmatites, 89
P-T-t paths, *see* Pressure-Temperature-time (P-T-t) paths

Q

quartz diorite orthogneisses, 36–37, *37*
QAP ternary diagram, 95–96

R

rapakivi texture, 95
rare earth element (REE), 96, 141, 143
Re-Os molybdenite chronometry, 92, 94, 107
retrograde metamorphism, 71–72, *72*
Roundstone Granite (RG), *63*
Roundstone Pluton, 98, 115, 120–122, *121*
Ryan, P.D., 98

S

Scandian Orogeny, 104, *104*
serpentinisation, 69
Shackleton, R.M., 45
Shannapheasteen Granite, 95, 109

Shannapheasteen Granodiorite (ShGr), 140
sillimanite, 61, *62*
Silurian Killary Harbour Formation, 5–6
Skird Rocks Fault (SRF), *106*, 107, 143
southern belt, 15; *see also* Metagabbro Gneiss Suite
    deformation phases, 47, *52*, 52–53, *53*
Southern Uplands Fault (SUF), *106*, 107
SRF, *see* Skird Rocks Fault
Sr-Nd isotopic model, 107, 109
Streamstown Connemara Marble Quarry, 45, *50–51*
Streamstown Schist Formation, 27, *30*, 67, 98
    Letterfrack Pluton, 122–123
    Omey Pluton, 116, *118*
    pelites and carbonates of, 119
    steep belt, 45
SUF, *see* Southern Uplands Fault
Sweeney, M., 157
syn-kinematic quartz diorite-granite magmatism, 79, *81*

T

Tanner, P.W.G., 19–20, 31–33, 45, 71, 98, 153
tectonic kinematic model, 103, 107, *108–109*
temporal emplacement model, 115
thermal metamorphism, 98, *99*

Tilley, C.C., 60
titanite-plagioclase ocelli, 137, *139*
Tourmakeady Volcanic Group, 54
Twelve Bens, 33, 45, *48–49*

U

UK and Irish Caledonian granites, 109, *110*
Unitt, R., 157
U-Pb geochronology, 56
U-Pb zircon system, 78, 92, 94, 107
Upper-Devonian granite magmas, 103–104, *105*, 109, *110*

V

Virtual Reality Modelling Language (VRML) models, 33
visualisation techniques, in Connemara, 33

W

western block, **132**, 133
Wilson, J.R., 131
Woodcock, N.H., 109
Wright, P.C., 129, 133

Y

Yardley, B.W.D., 71, 78, 85, *86*, 87, 89, 98

For Product Safety Concerns and Information please contact our
EU representative GPSR@taylorandfrancis.com Taylor & Francis
Verlag GmbH, Kaufingerstraße 24, 80331 München, Germany